trauma-sensitive instruction

creating a safe and predictable classroom environment

JOHN F. ELLER & TOM HIERCK

Solution Tree | Press
a division of Solution Tree

555 North Morton Street
Bloomington, IN 47404
800.733.6786 (toll free) / 812.336.7700
FAX: 812.336.7790

email: info@SolutionTree.com
SolutionTree.com

Visit **go.SolutionTree.com/behavior** to download the free reproducibles in this book.

Printed in the United States of America

FSC
www.fsc.org
MIX
Paper from responsible sources
FSC® C011935

Library of Congress Cataloging-in-Publication Data

Names: Eller, John, 1957- author. | Hierck, Tom, 1960- author.
Title: Trauma-sensitive instruction : creating a safe and predictable classroom environment / John F. Eller, Tom Hierck.
Description: Bloomington, IN : Solution Tree Press, 2021. | Includes bibliographical references and index.
Identifiers: LCCN 2021006606 (print) | LCCN 2021006607 (ebook) | ISBN 9781949539950 (paperback) | ISBN 9781949539967 (ebook)
Subjects: LCSH: Children with mental disabilities--Education. | Psychic trauma in children. | Post-traumatic stress disorder in children. | Classroom environment--Psychological aspects.
Classification: LCC LC4165 .E45 2021 (print) | LCC LC4165 (ebook) | DDC 371.94--dc23
LC record available at https://lccn.loc.gov/2021006606
LC ebook record available at https://lccn.loc.gov/2021006607

Solution Tree
Jeffrey C. Jones, CEO
Edmund M. Ackerman, President

Solution Tree Press
President and Publisher: Douglas M. Rife
Associate Publisher: Sarah Payne-Mills
Art Director: Rian Anderson
Managing Production Editor: Kendra Slayton
Copy Chief: Jessi Finn
Senior Production Editor: Christine Hood
Content Development Specialist: Amy Rubenstein
Copy Editor: Kate St. Ives
Proofreader: Evie Madsen
Editorial Assistants: Sarah Ludwig and Elijah Oates

Dedication

Writing and developing this book during the COVID-19 pandemic has strengthened our connection to families, friends, and colleagues. We would like to dedicate this book to our wives, Sheila Eller and Ingrid Hierck. Both of you have provided infinite support and encouragement during this process. As sounding boards to the content, you provided invaluable assistance. As spouses who have helped us with our growth and supported us during the difficult moments, your value is immeasurable. Without your energy, this project would not have been possible. Thank you!

Thanks to our children, Michael, Matt, and Michelle Eller, and Kristin, David, and Shannon Hierck. While we raised you, you taught us how to be good parents and listeners. You inspire and motivate us. Thank you for the gifts you have given us over the years. As grandparents, we are also exposed to many opportunities to learn from those young hearts. John thanks Everett and Brooks, and Tom thanks Isabella, Leah, Liam, Kaiden, Wren, and Bodhi. We strive to be the kinds of adults our grandchildren think we are.

Since we have made the journey from childhood trauma to resilient adults, we want to thank those teachers who reached out and helped us when we were growing up. Over the years, we have had a chance to thank some of them personally for what they did to help and support us. Unfortunately, some of them passed on before we had the chance. They may not have known how their small efforts impacted us when we most needed it. Thanks for caring!

Finally, we want to thank the many teachers and school leaders who are working in schools every day, lifting up trauma-impacted students and helping them build resilience. Your work is difficult, but you are making a difference, one child at a time. Thank you for what you are doing to develop the next group of adults who will break the cycle of trauma with their own children and other children they impact.

Acknowledgments

Although only two names appear on the cover, this book would not be possible without the support and input of many colleagues and friends.

Beginning with our Solution Tree family, we would like to thank the following key supporters: Jeff Jones, who built a company that encourages educators to find their voice and share with colleagues; Douglas Rife, the president and publisher of Solution Tree Press, who provided us with the opportunity and encouragement to develop and write the book; Christine Hood, our senior editor, who helped refine the rough manuscript into a book that flows and make sense for busy teachers; Kate St. Ives, our copy editor; Evie Madsen, our proofreader; Rian Anderson, our cover and text designer, who created the colorful and engaging cover that conveys the central message of the book; and Shik Love and Kelly Rockhill, whose skills in marketing and promotion will ensure this book reaches a wide audience and can have the maximum benefit to colleagues.

Additional members of the Solution Tree team who worked diligently to support our work and refine the content include Sarah Payne-Mills, associate publisher; Amy Rubenstein, content development specialist; and Kendra Slayton, managing production editor.

We would also like to acknowledge the following mentors and supporters who have inspired us, provided encouragement and direction, as well as feedback on our efforts. Jim Sporleder, the former principal of Lincoln School, who has lived the elements and strategies presented in this book; Paulette Carter, whose experiences with Hurricane Katrina and her vast knowledge of trauma and resilience helped to shape the content; and Earl Moulton, whose experience in police services provided some key insights and whose willingness to share ideas helped to hone the book you are about to read.

Solution Tree Press would like to thank the following reviewer:

Stephen Guenrich
Principal
Paragould Junior High School
Paragould, Arkansas

Table of Contents

About the Authors

John F. Eller, PhD, is a former principal, director of a principals' training center, and assistant superintendent for curriculum, learning, and staff development.

John is also a much sought-after consultant to schools and school districts both nationally and internationally. He specializes in trauma-informed teaching and leadership, school turnaround, dealing with difficult people, building professional learning communities, conducting employee evaluations, building conferencing and coaching skills, developing strategic planning strategies, building supervisory skills, and implementing effective teaching strategies. John also serves as a consultant for U.S. federal government agencies on the topics of team building, conflict coaching, peer coaching, conflict resolution, employee evaluations, and performance reviews, leadership, and a variety of other pertinent topics supporting U.S. federal employees and leaders.

John has written and cowritten numerous articles and books, including a two-year series supporting new principals for the NAESP publication, *Principal,* and *Effective Group Facilitation in Education, Working With and Evaluating Difficult School Employees, So Now You're the Superintendent!, Energizing Staff Meetings, Creative Strategies to Transform School Culture, Thriving as a New Teacher, Score to Soar, Achieving Great Impact, Working With Difficult and Resistant Staff,* and *Flip This School.*

John earned a doctorate in educational leadership and policy studies from Loyola University Chicago and a master's degree in educational leadership from the University of Nebraska Omaha.

To learn more about John's work, visit his website at ellerandassociaties.com, or follow him @jellerthree on Twitter.

Tom Hierck has been an educator since 1983 in a career that has spanned all grade levels and many roles in public education. His experiences as a teacher, an administrator, a district leader, a department of education project leader, and an executive director provide a unique context for his education philosophy.

Tom is a compelling presenter, infusing his message of hope with strategies culled from the real world. He understands that educators face unprecedented challenges and knows which strategies will best serve learning communities. Tom has presented to schools and districts across North America with a message of celebration for educators seeking to make a difference in the lives of students. His dynamic presentations explore the importance of positive learning environments and the role of assessment to improve student learning. Tom's belief that "every student is a success story waiting to be told" has led him to work with teachers and administrators to create positive school cultures and build effective relationships that facilitate learning for all students.

To learn more about Tom's work, visit his website at tomhierck.com, or follow him @thierck on Twitter or Tom Hierck on Facebook.

To book John F. Eller or Tom Hierck for professional development, contact pd@SolutionTree.com.

Introduction

Brittany is a sophomore in high school. She comes from a home where her mom is the head of the household. Her dad is no longer involved in her life. There are many days Brittany comes to school after experiencing a stressful morning with her mom and her siblings.

Brittany's teacher, Ms. Smith, has made significant changes to her classroom. She has taught her students how the brain functions and how to monitor themselves so they know when they are experiencing stress. When students start to feel stress, they can go to special places in the classroom to reflect and work toward getting calmer. Ms. Smith greets all her students when they enter the classroom and makes mental notes about what she has observed that may help her understand their moods. She doesn't press them or make them tell her what may be bothering them, but she is nearby when they need support. When a behavior problem occurs, Ms. Smith tries to understand what may have triggered it rather than reacting and punishing students.

As a result of Ms. Smith's techniques and support, Brittany feels that she is accepted for who she is, and that Ms. Smith has her back as she is trying to learn and grow.

In this brief example, Brittany's teacher has implemented strategies to help her students experience a safe classroom where they can get away from the daily adverse experiences they have to deal with in their homes and neighborhoods. Educators have no control over the homes students come from. You need to stop lamenting and start building capacity when those students come to *your house*—that is, your school.

Think about your school as a home that strives to develop the essential skills needed for *all* students to reach their fullest potential. It's the house you can control and the house where you can build positive routines that allow students to become their own unique success stories. The classroom environment helps set the tone and nurture a culture where students can learn how to work toward positive mental health and develop resiliency to handle stress and manage behaviors.

While Ms. Smith ensures her classroom is a supportive and accepting place, it is not a place of anything-goes behavior. She helps students deal with issues and misbehaviors while maintaining a sound classroom environment. Ms. Smith knows which issues need to be addressed immediately and which issues can be postponed until the student has had a chance to get his or her emotions under control.

Even though trauma-informed instruction seems relatively new, the concepts grounding it are not new. M. Shelley Thomas, Shantel Crosby, and Judi Vanderhaar (2019) identified trauma in the 1860s when soldiers returned from war. For a number of years, trauma treatment was confined to clinical settings, support groups, and the like (Thomas et al., 2019). Youth trauma and its importance became more prominent, in part, due to the work of Vincent J. Felitti (2019), which focused on how childhood trauma (*adverse childhood experiences,* or ACEs) affects the health of adults. As we explore in chapter 1 (page 13), there is consensus around the idea that childhood trauma has long-lasting impact on the health of adults. The awareness of the impact of trauma outside the school setting has made educators look beyond simple causes behind misbehaviors and try to determine if trauma outside of school influences behaviors that may be visible in school.

In working to understand the situations some of your students face, it may be hard, as an educator, to feel how difficult these situations may be and how hard it is to concentrate. Later, as we examine how the human brain typically responds to trauma and stress, you'll see how the entire cognitive process can be shut down or taken hostage when a child is trying to cope with a traumatic experience.

In our work over the years supporting educators dealing with trauma in their students, some have shared comments such as, "I don't understand why he acts out like this," or "Why doesn't she feel she can share her situation with me? I think we have a good relationship." Many of these same educators also told us they grew up in pretty safe and stable homes. They said they did not have to worry about a drunk parent coming home and beating them up or coming home to an empty house and having to take care of their siblings because their parent is out partying.

Educators need to consider what students are experiencing in their traumatic situations. It is an advantage for you if you can empathize with them; in doing so, you walk in their shoes. Pairing the strategies and techniques of developing trauma-sensitive instruction with the ability to try to understand the trauma is a powerful combination for working successfully with trauma-impacted students; it is a true empathic effort.

Understanding the impact of trauma can help teachers develop safe and predictable classrooms. Safe and predictable classrooms can help decrease disruptions and help students focus and do better in school. These teachers understand the importance of considering sound mental health practices in their classrooms. We'll focus on the impact of trauma and sound mental health practices in this book.

Our Personal Experiences With Childhood Trauma and Mental Health

Because of our backgrounds and experiences, we are uniquely qualified to assist teachers and school leaders as they work with children from traumatic homes and situations. Our biographies appear inside the front of this book, but following are some of the experiences we've had to directly transfer to the mission of supporting students, teachers, and school leaders in working with trauma-impacted students. In addition to our practical experiences in teaching and leading trauma-informed settings, we have also personally experienced childhood trauma ourselves.

John F. Eller

John grew up in the Midwest in a blue-collar family where alcoholism, violence, and poverty had been multigenerational. John knew the situation he was in was not the norm, and that other children were not experiencing the same things he was experiencing. As a young child, John saw the effects of alcoholism and aggression in his parents' and family members' behaviors. He learned how to cope with these situations and developed resiliency to tackle the difficult experiences he faced.

A few of John's teachers provided him with sound and nurturing classrooms, so he felt safe. School became a respite from the situations at home and further helped John develop a sound mental perspective and survive his situation.

John's response to the situation was not shared by others in the home. His brother, unfortunately, was unable to overcome the challenges of his background. The result was two different adults. John learned to manage stress and not pass on the same dysfunctional behaviors to his children, while his brother has spent time in prison, abused drugs, and has had a much more difficult life. John was able to overcome the trauma and focus on improving his life, while his brother was not. What made the difference? John developed resilience, while his brother did not.

In developing this book, John called on his extensive experiences in implementing foundational strategies that support trauma-informed classrooms and schools, plus his research and previous writings related to the topic.

John has served as an elementary and a secondary school teacher, a principal in several schools, an assistant superintendent of curriculum and learning, a principals' center director, a university professor, and various other positions during his career. John's experiences include the following.

- Worked extensively as a classroom teacher, principal, and district office administrator in communities and neighborhoods that serve students living in traumatic conditions.
- Supported teachers and leaders as a consultant in the areas of positive classroom environments, classroom management, building relationships, developing parent partnerships, and other areas directly related to ACEs.
- Developed and implemented programs that were beneficial to students experiencing trauma. One of his schools was honored with the Iowa First in the National Education (FINE) Award, an award for transforming school culture; and John was named the state principal of the year and a National Distinguished Principal by the U.S. Department of Education.
- Authored many books and articles on topics related to trauma-informed instruction, including developing the *care factor* with students and families, in which the principal helps teachers and students feel

that someone cares for them; in turn, teachers show their level of caring for students, and then students show each other they care. This helps establish and maintain a caring and nurturing school culture. Topics also include school culture, classroom management, de-escalating conflict, and working with teachers to implement change.

- Worked as a consultant since 1996 with schools, districts, intermediate education agencies, and other education institutions on foundational topics related to trauma-informed classrooms and schools. In addition to consulting on these topics in North America, John also has worked with teachers and leaders in Chile, Australia, China, Japan, and Europe.

Tom Hierck

Tom grew up in the eastern part of Canada in the province of Quebec. As one of eight children of parents who emigrated from the Netherlands, his childhood was not the stuff one might positively associate with a family in which everyone supports the greater good. The physical and mental abuse impacted every member of the family and was compounded by a lack of financial security. Family members never discussed their situation with anyone outside the home, and on the surface all seemed normal.

In his early school career, Tom was not motivated and seemed destined to follow in the footsteps of his older siblings. A lack of achievement was the norm in Tom's family. Being the class clown was his objective at the time. Without much supportive structure in the home, Tom sought that support in places and spaces away from home. School was his first place of respite with significant adults who looked beyond the clown charade and found the person hiding behind it—teachers in the truest sense of the word.

In a family of eight, the responses to trauma by each family member were as varied as his or her personality and individual strengths. Three did not survive the choices they made. For Tom, the goal became one of working to make the life in front of him better than the life behind him, to not continue a pattern of dysfunction that is often easily repeated. It was about ensuring that his future offspring, and the generations that followed, were not tagged with the heavy burden of that dysfunction.

Tom has channeled all his expertise and experiences into this new book to help teachers and leaders make their classrooms more trauma informed. Tom has served as a teacher, a school administrator, a program director, and an author in the area of trauma-informed teaching and leading. Tom's experiences include the following.

- Worked extensively as a teacher, an administrator, and a consultant in the areas of trauma, behavior management, and developing student resilience and potential.
- Worked in programs serving students with severe behavior issues and in alternative education programs designed to help students experiencing trauma.
- Developed a model program to help indigenous students and families.
- Led the reform of a behavior program that helped students build resilience, and implemented intervention programs, such as positive behavioral interventions and supports (PBIS), to help teachers understand the trauma behind behaviors and teach students alternative behaviors while building resilience.
- Worked as a consultant in North American and Australia helping educators understand student trauma, building classrooms and schools that are more trauma sensitive, developing classroom environments where students are taught and practice productive behaviors, building positive learning environments, and championing the idea that *all* students can learn and be successful at high levels.
- Authored many books on response to intervention (RTI), school and classroom culture, assessment, and positive behavior management all related to trauma-sensitive teaching and leading.

Both of us have had experiences similar to those many of your students may have experienced. This has been a tremendous asset in our work with children from traumatic situations. These experiences have helped us *relate* to them and understand some of what they are going through themselves, allowing us to empathize and step back and try to understand each situation in a unique manner.

Some of you may also have experienced trauma as a child. Somehow, you may have overcome your situation, or maybe the experiences are hidden in your deep memory and may influence how you think and process experiences. Your experiences may have made you more sensitive and aware of the impact of trauma on your students, or they may have made you less tolerant of some of the situations your students are facing. This lack of tolerance may lead someone to think, "I worked hard and overcame my traumatic situations, why can't my students do the same?" In contrast, if your experiences have made you too sensitive, you may allow your students too much leeway so that they are unaccountable for their behaviors. Letting students get by with misbehaviors does not help them develop the resilience they need in order to overcome their trauma.

As we work to support teachers and leaders, many tell us that they are seeing more and more students impacted by trauma and mental health challenges. We have observed how trauma-impacted students struggle to focus and learn. These issues impact classroom and behavior management, and cause teachers to take time away from teaching and learning activities to address students' mental health needs.

You don't need to have experienced childhood trauma to try to empathize and understand your students' perspectives. If you try to understand what your students might be experiencing, that's a great first step. Being able to step back before reacting will help you better understand their situations and develop positive relationships to help you work with them more successfully.

Purpose of This Book

You may wonder, "Why write a book on trauma-informed instruction?" As we work with educators in a variety of settings, we've noticed that more and more of them are dealing with children who come from homes where traumatic experiences are a regular occurrence. John worked with a school district in the Midwest in which the quiet of the neighborhood was interrupted by violence and gunshots on a nightly basis. Tom worked in an indigenous community where students are impacted by isolation, poverty, lack of meaningful employment, and alcoholism. These two situations can cause stress and trauma that students bring with them to their schools and classrooms.

As good as the educators may be in these two example settings, to help students learn and grow, they are equally challenged to find ways to help students become successful adults. These educators are hungry for ideas and strategies to help their students overcome their challenges and achieve both in and out of the classroom.

Since we both have experienced childhood trauma, worked to overcome its impacts, and have successfully helped students experiencing trauma, we decided to share our experiences so others can benefit from what we've seen and learned. This book is the culmination of our personal and professional experiences with trauma, resilience, mental health, school culture, and a myriad of other topics we have addressed as teachers, instructional leaders, and consultants since we began our careers in the early 1980s.

The book also contains research-proven and time-tested strategies and techniques to help positively impact the effects of trauma. These strategies will give you a well-rounded foundation to build on in your classroom.

Increase in Trauma and Mental Health Needs

As educators working every day with students, you know about the increased incidents of students experiencing trauma and mental health challenges in your classrooms. The pressures and mental health challenges posed by students in crisis can take up valuable time that might be better dedicated to academic learning. These challenges can range from students who seem withdrawn and disconnected, to those who disrupt the learning of others. Janie Crecco (2017) outlined the original ACEs study and described childhood trauma as *America's hidden health crisis.* Thomas and her colleagues (2019) note, "This work sheds light on the importance of preventing childhood trauma and also recognizing and addressing the needs of youth exposed to adverse events prior to their journey into adulthood" (p. 424).

The topic of ACEs came to light in the 1990s with a study cosponsored by the Centers for Disease Control and Prevention (CDC) and the health insurance company, Kaiser Permanente (CDC, 2020a). This study examined the early experiences of approximately 17,000 middle-class adults. The study participants were asked to respond to a questionnaire asking them to identify their experiences with adverse, stressful situations. The initial ACEs survey included experiences such as substance abuse in the home, parent incarceration, neglect of basic needs, and others (for more information, see www.cdc/gov.violenceprevention/aces/about.html).

The initial results of the original ACEs study are staggering. Almost 25 percent of the study participants had experienced two or more of the adverse experiences listed. More than one in sixteen had experienced four or more of the adverse experiences. Among the adults who participated in the study, those with higher ACEs scores also had more health challenges. Truly, their childhood experiences impacted their lives as adults (CDC, 2020a).

Since the problem of childhood stress and mental health challenges is getting larger and more pronounced, additional studies on children have been conducted. Data from the National Survey of Children's Health from 2011–2012 (as cited in Lu, 2017) shows that nearly 35 million children experience at least one source of stress. Helen L. Egger and Adrian Angold (2006) find that children between the ages of two and five experience at least one type of severe stressor in their lifetime. Researchers and mental health professionals are concerned about the high numbers of children experiencing at least one stressful situation but are even more concerned about those experiencing multiple stressors. According to Salvatore Terrasi and Patricia Crain de Galarce (2017), "Children who live in a consistently dysfunctional environment often manifest symptoms of what has become known as *complex trauma,* which is the cumulative effect of traumatic experiences that are repeated or prolonged over time" (p. 36).

Limited Resources Available to Teachers

While there are many books and resources available to help teachers improve their instructional strategies, there are few resources to help teachers to understand and impact trauma. In many cases, teachers are told to do their best or be understanding when instructional strategies are not enough. Teachers are also focused on the academic achievement of *all* students and don't have the time or training necessary to provide the counseling some students need to cope with their traumatic situations.

In this book, we share research-based and classroom-proven practices that can help establish and maintain a classroom environment that not only helps students experiencing trauma be successful but also all students.

Overview of This Book

This book focuses on helping you understand the impact of trauma and how you can refine your classroom to minimize its impact. It includes some foundational information to assist you in understanding the background of trauma and also contains practical, time-tested strategies to help you establish a classroom environment that is sensitive and trauma informed. By *trauma informed,* we mean keeping the needs of trauma-impacted students at the forefront of your planning and decision making. Considering trauma-impacted students will help ensure that your classroom provides a safe environment to help students deal with the immediate impacts of trauma while building resilience to better handle future trauma in their lives.

This book offers practical strategies you can immediately implement in your classroom, along with real-world scenarios describing how teachers face and deal with trauma-impacted students and their families. Although these scenarios are based on real situations, people's and schools' names have been changed to protect their privacy. Skip around and feel free to read and learn about those ideas you think will be most beneficial to your classroom, your students, and your teaching. You may choose to start in the middle of the book, at the end, or anywhere else most beneficial to you. Some of the activities and strategies may require sequential steps for implementation, while others may not. Choose what's best for you.

As you find promising ideas and strategies, examine them and how they could fit into your existing practices. If you can look at what you're already doing and refine those practices, you'll find changing to become trauma informed will be an easier journey. The new ideas will be more natural and easier to implement.

When you begin to tackle major changes in your practice, be sure you understand each change and how it will help your students experience success. You may want to invite other colleagues to go on the journey with you. After all, there's motivation in numbers. Then develop a plan for these major changes that includes follow-up support and coaching. As you implement these new strategies, you may encounter periodic setbacks. While setbacks are normal, they can be discouraging and slow down your progress. Don't get discouraged, as change always takes time.

The chapters in this book are designed to provide a step-by-step process for understanding ourselves as educators, childhood trauma and its impact on mental health, and strategies to positively impact students in your classroom. Following is an overview of the information you will find in each chapter.

- **Chapter 1: The Impact of Trauma on Educators and Students—** Chapter 1 presents a concise but important overview of the presence and impact of traumatic situations, including how trauma impacts the brain. This information will help you develop a mindset for the situations you face and provide a rationale for convincing you, colleagues, administrators, and students' parents why you are making changes in your classroom. The rationale, and understanding the importance of your work, will help keep you moving forward when you face setbacks and challenges while implementing new techniques and strategies.

- **Chapter 2: The Importance of Attitude and Mindset in Working With Trauma**—Thinking about what some students face and selecting an attitude in working with trauma-impacted students is crucial to your success in helping them. In this chapter, you'll examine strategies and techniques you can use to ensure you have a positive and helpful mindset and attitude.
- **Chapter 3: Classroom Structures to Support Trauma-Sensitive Practices**—The first place you'll want to start your work is providing a safe and nurturing, yet structured, learning environment. This chapter shows how you can create a classroom environment and culture to serve as the foundation for your success in working with trauma and mental health issues.
- **Chapter 4: Positive Relationships With Students**—Sound, meaningful, and appropriate relationships are another base or foundation for success with students experiencing trauma. Many of these students lack the important relationships they need for good personal mental health because of their traumatic situations. In this chapter, you'll learn how to build these important relationships.
- **Chapter 5: Trauma-Sensitive Classroom Management Strategies and Techniques**—Teachers sometimes see the effects of trauma play out in disruptive behaviors in their classrooms. Students experiencing trauma don't always respond positively to traditional authoritarian management strategies. Students do respond to strategies that maximize consistency, which helps them learn how to identify triggers that may set off misbehavior. They also benefit from learning how to develop good behavior habits that help them get their needs met. In this chapter, you'll learn how to implement classroom management systems that reduce confrontation and build good learning behavior habits.

- **Chapter 6: Parent and Family Engagement**—The family that might be causing the traumatic situation is also the family that is key to working positively with the student. Building a supportive and trusting relationship with students' families not only helps you understand the situation but it may also help you influence part of that environment to make it more stable for the student. In this chapter, you'll learn a variety of productive ways to build partnerships with students' families so you can work together to ensure student success.

As you move forward on your journey working with trauma-impacted students, we hope the chapters in this book will provide positive and productive strategies you can be comfortable and confident implementing in your classroom. This journey may take some time, but it will be productive time as you improve the lives of your students and move them toward success both inside and outside of the classroom.

chapter one

The Impact of Trauma on Educators and Students

Thelma keeps to herself in the classroom. She rarely answers questions or participates in class discussions. When her teacher, Mr. Jackson, tries to talk with her, she avoids eye contact and is evasive in answering his questions. Even though she doesn't seem to enjoy school, she stays around at the end of the day, looking for things to do and delaying her walk home.

Mr. Jackson is concerned that she is unconnected and withdrawn. When he speaks to other teachers who had Thelma in their classes in past years, they remember her as energetic and engaged. Thelma seemed to change shortly after her parents separated in the spring. Mr. Jackson is concerned and wants to find a way to help Thelma.

In this example, Thelma exhibits behaviors that are distancing her from her teachers and peers. No one knows for sure, but the situation with her parents could be impacting her and her behavior in the classroom.

We work with students who face pressures and traumas outside the classroom. Societal pressures have increased, more students are living in poverty, violence and conflict are promoted through the media and social media, and other pressures increase the chance for students to experience trauma at an early age.

A large part of your students' lives occur outside of school and are out of your direct control, but you need to be able to recognize the impact of childhood trauma and make your classroom more trauma sensitive.

As educators become more aware of the trauma children experience in their lives, it is essential that they have an understanding of childhood trauma and how they can lessen its impact in classrooms. As you review the information in this chapter, be sure to focus on the following.

- Definitions of *trauma* and *complex trauma* and how these conditions impact students and classrooms
- Statistics that illustrate the prevalence of childhood trauma in society
- The nature of the brain and the way trauma impacts children's brains
- The impacts of trauma on the brain and how the brain responds in various traumatic situations
- An awareness of your own potential to experience early childhood trauma and how those experiences might taint or color your ability to work with students who experience trauma in their own lives

Educators all see the impacts of trauma and traumatic experiences on the students they work with on a daily basis. Teachers tell us they see more and more students who appear to be impacted by trauma in their classrooms. "The CDC has deemed ACE a major public health issue, rightfully so, as we see the impacts of childhood trauma in our classrooms nationally. In addition, childhood trauma that goes unresolved in the adults in our educational system also impacts our classrooms" (Nealy-Oparah & Scruggs-Hussein, 2018, pp. 12–13).

It's easy to imagine that the COVID-19 pandemic, which began in 2020 and resulted in massive increases in unemployment, virtual learning, and other impacts, will add more stress to families and children in schools. Increasing your awareness and implementing strategies to make your classroom more trauma sensitive can provide students with a safe environment in which to learn and grow.

Trauma Defined

Childhood trauma can set the tone for difficulties in school. Kathleen Fitzgerald Rice and Betsy McAlister Groves (2005) offer the following definition of *trauma*: "Trauma is an exceptional experience in which powerful and dangerous events overwhelm a person's capacity to cope" (p. 3). The preceding definition contains key descriptors that communicate the impact of trauma, including *exceptional*, *powerful*, *dangerous*, and *overwhelm*. All these terms taken together convey the sense that some of your students' experiences are well outside the boundaries of normal.

The impact of trauma can be different for each person. Trauma is an emotional experience that directly impacts each student in a slightly different manner but has a definite and lasting impact on learning. Kristin Souers and Pete Hall (2016) point out, "Our own interpretations influence the degree of impact we feel following exposure to a traumatic event" (p. 16).

This important fact should help teachers shape how they interact with trauma-impacted students. Many students come from homes and neighborhoods where stressful and traumatic experiences are regular occurrences. For example, according to Souers and Hall (2016), "A report of child abuse is made every 10 seconds" (p. 19). Since the frequency of abuse is so common, many students must not have stable home environments due to experiences from direct abuse and neglect and other situations in which there is constant stress. Teachers tell us that the constant stress and lack of stability set up students for difficulties in calming down in order to feel safe and learn. Following are just some of the traumatic scenarios our teacher colleagues have reported students have told them about or they have discovered in trying to help students learn.

- Neighborhood violence
- Homelessness
- Single parent homes (Living in a single-parent home itself may not cause stress, but complications, such as the parent holding more than one job, experiencing economic difficulties, dating, and other factors, may contribute to student stress.)
- A parent in prison
- Left home alone to take care of things while parents are gone
- Physical or emotional abuse
- Excessive responsibility for sibling care
- Observation of drug abuse
- Violence of one parent against another
- Multiple families living in the same home (Multiple families living in the same home itself may not cause stress and trauma, but aspects such as lack of privacy, no dedicated study environment, potential conflicts that may occur because of crowded living spaces, and other issues, may contribute to student stress and trauma.)

- The victim of bullying
- In foster care
- Gang recruitment and gang violence

These and other traumatic events and scenarios cause students to be on constant watch for their own safely. When they are worrying about and reacting to violent environments or the fear of violence, it's hard for them to be able to relax and concentrate on thinking and learning.

This situation is bad for students experiencing a small number of traumatic situations, but children in extended traumatic situations can develop what Jim Sporleder and Heather T. Forbes (2016) refer to as *toxic stress*. Toxic stress can lead to issues that can impair students' normal development and success in the classroom. In reference students and toxic stress, Sporleder and Forbes (2016) state:

> Their bodies remain in activation mode (fight-flight-freeze). Stress activates the body's psychological response with increased levels of stress hormone . . . excessive exposure to is harmful because the body continues to pump out high levels of stress hormones which then become toxic to the human body. The cumulative result of this over-activated stress-response system in the context of chronic adversity is known as toxic stress. (p. 20)

Toxic stress is harmful for everyone but especially for children. You may see this impact reflected in students' attention span and classroom behavior. "Most children coming out of toxic environments will show signs of developmental deficits and, unfortunately, this can easily be misrepresented as 'bad' or 'negative' behavior" (Sporleder & Forbes, 2016, p. 21).

Let's see how the impact of trauma influences Laura, a middle school student dealing with a traumatic home life, even when she is not in the traumatic situation.

> *Laura, a seventh-grade student, lives in a home where her father drinks excessively and comes home drunk. When he gets home, he is both verbally and physically abusive to Laura's mom and any of the children he sees. Laura normally knows that when he comes home, it's a good idea to stay out of his way and try to be invisible. She usually withdraws from the situation and tries not to cause a lot of issues.*
>
> *In her classes, Laura uses similar behavior. Even though she may not understand what she is learning, she is reluctant to ask questions or*

get clarification. When working in groups, Laura contributes little to the conversation and goes along with the ideas of the group. She is reluctant to make eye contact with people (adults and peers) and appears to be disconnected and isolated.

Even though Laura is not exhibiting violent behaviors, her behavior has been impacted by her traumatic situation. In the short term, her traumatic home situation is negatively impacting her opportunities to learn and grow. As the home situation continues, her physical and emotional health could be impacted. In a safe and supportive classroom environment, Laura may build resilience and find ways to overcome the impacts of the situation.

Original ACEs Study and Continued Prevalence of the Problem

The impact of trauma is something that teachers may have thought about for years. When we were students, it may have that seemed our teachers had information about our backgrounds and tried to provide positive experiences to counteract the trauma at home.

For example, when John was in seventh grade, one of his teachers invited him to join a fishing club. This teacher helped John get his first fishing pole and took him fishing. This experience gave John some temporary respite from his traumatic home experiences.

During this time in John's life, he did not share these traumatic experiences with others outside the immediate family. Most of the time, John felt he was all alone. Certainly, he never heard any of his peers or friends talk about these kinds of experiences. Traumatic family issues were kept private and hidden from others.

Even though some teachers were able to intervene, there was no comprehensive understanding of the impact of traumatic experiences on children or adults. There was very little understanding of the problem or the impacts of the problem.

As noted previously in the introduction (see page 8), in the late 1990s, scientists began to examine the effects of childhood trauma on adult health. The CDC and Department of Preventative Medicine in San Diego conducted a collaborative research study that examined approximately 17,000 subjects identified as middle class adults (CDC, 2020a). Participants received a survey, which included a list of ten traumatic events. They were asked to rate which events they experienced before age eighteen. These traumatic events were called *adverse childhood experiences* (ACEs). The original list of these ACEs includes the following (CDC, 2020a):

- Abuse
    - **Emotional abuse:** A parent, stepparent, or adult living in your home swore at you, insulted you, put you down, or acted in a way that made you afraid that you might be physically hurt.
    - **Physical abuse:** A parent, stepparent, or adult living in your home pushed, grabbed, slapped, threw something at you, or hit you so hard that you had marks or were injured.
    - **Sexual abuse:** An adult, relative, family friend, or stranger who was at least 5 years older than you touched or fondled your body in a sexual way, made you touch his or her body in a sexual way, attempted to have any type of sexual intercourse with you.
- Household challenges
    - **Mother treated violently:** Your mother or stepmother was pushed, grabbed, slapped, had something thrown at her, kicked, bitten, hit with a fist, hit with something hard, repeatedly hit for over at least a few minutes, or was at any time threatened or hurt by a knife or gun by your father (or stepfather) or mother's boyfriend.
    - **Substance abuse in the household:** A household member was a problem drinker or alcoholic or a household member used street drugs.
    - **Mental illness in the household:** A household member was depressed or mentally ill or a household member attempted suicide.
    - **Parental separation or divorce:** Your parents were ever separated or divorced.
    - **Incarcerated household member:** A household member went to prison.
- Neglect
    - **Emotional neglect:** [Nobody] in your family helped you feel important or special . . . [or] loved, people in your family [did not look] out for each other or [feel] close to each other, your family was [not] a source of strength and support.

- **Physical neglect:** There was [nobody] to take care of you, protect you, and take you to the doctor if you needed it, you didn't have enough to eat, your parents were too drunk or too high to take care of you, and you had to wear dirty clothes.

The results were surprising. Of the 17,000 people in the study group, almost 25 percent reported that they had experienced multiple (more than one) ACEs. One in sixteen people in the study group reported that they had experienced four or more ACEs (CDC, 2020a).

The original ACE study was mainly designed to examine relationships between adverse childhood experiences and adult-level health issues. The high prevalence of ACEs in the adults in the study may have been surprising to some people.

Since the original ACEs study, there have been follow-up studies directly related to children. Here is some of the information from follow-up studies.

- Nearly 35 million U.S. children have experienced at least one type of childhood trauma (Lu, 2017).
- Egger and Angold (2006) found children ages two to five had experienced at least one severe stressor in their lives.
- "Whether they work in a rural, urban, or suburban district . . . more than half of the students enrolled in public schools have faced traumatic or adverse experiences and one in six struggles with complex trauma" (Felitti & Anda, 2009, as cited in Terrasi & de Galarce, 2017).

Schools, teachers, and school leaders we work with found value in taking the ACEs questionnaire to determine their own ACEs score. The original questionnaire used in the CDC study (2020a) included questions related to the health of the respondents since the study was examining longer-term health impacts related to ACEs. (Visit www.cdc.gov/violenceprevention/aces/about.html to access the full ACEs survey.)

Figure 1.1 (page 20) features an adapted version of the original questionnaire, focusing only on the ACEs components.

Adverse Childhood Experience Questionnaire

Please review the following questions. Respond *yes* if this situation happened to you during your childhood (up to age eighteen) or *no* if it did not.

1. Did a parent or other adult in the household often . . .

Swear at you, insult you, put you down, or humiliate you?

Or

Act in a way that made you afraid that you might be physically hurt?

NO _____ YES _____

2. Did a parent or another adult in the household often . . .

Push, grab, slap, or throw something at you?

Or

Ever hit you so hard that you had marks or were injured?

NO _____ YES _____

3. Did an adult or a person at least five years older than you ever . . .

Touch or fondle you or have you touch his or her body in a sexual way?

Or

Try to or actually have oral, anal, or vaginal sex with you?

NO _____ YES _____

4. Did you often feel that . . .

No one in your family loved you or thought you were important or special?

Or

Your family didn't look out for each other, feel close to each other, or support each other?

NO _____ YES _____

5. Did you often feel that . . .

You didn't have enough to eat, had to wear dirty clothes, and had no one to protect you?

Or

Your parents were too drunk or high to take care of you or take you to the doctor if you needed it?

NO _____ YES _____

6. Were your parents ever separated or divorced?

NO _____ YES _____

7. Was your mother or stepmother . . . Often pushed, grabbed, slapped, or had something thrown at her? Or Sometimes kicked, bitten, hit with a fist, or hit with something hard? Or Repeatedly hit for at least a few minutes or threatened with a gun or knife? NO _____ YES _____
8. Did you live with anyone who was a problem drinker or alcoholic or used street drugs? NO _____ YES _____
9. Was a household member depressed or mentally ill, or did a household member attempt suicide? NO _____ YES _____
10. Did a household member go to prison? NO _____ YES _____
Your ACEs Score For all of the *yes* responses, score each one as a +1. Total up all of your + 1 scores. That number is your ACEs score. TOTAL *YES* RESPONSES: _____

Source: Adapted from Centers for Disease Control and Prevention, 2020a.

Figure 1.1: Adverse childhood experiences questionnaire.

Impacts of Trauma on the Brain

Earlier in this text, we presented information about the impact of stress and multiple traumatic situations on children. As Sporleder and Forbes (2016) point out, the increased levels of stress-related hormones is negative for learners. In *Fostering Resilient Learners,* Souers and Hall (2016) add to this understanding of stress and its impact on students: "Quite plainly, I believe if our students aren't in the *learning mode*—a term coined by Pete's mentor, Frank C. Garrity, that refers to mental, physical, emotional, spiritual, and psychological readiness to learn—they simply will not learn" (pp. 26–27).

It is critical for educators to understand the impact of trauma on students' brains and how they can help children to move past this impact and increase their ıg. In the next section, we will discuss basic functions of the brain to aide in nderstanding.

In order to understand the impact of trauma on students, it's important to understand basic brain structure and function. In *Unlimited Power,* Anthony Robbins (1986) discusses the idea that human brains have a couple of basic responsibilities: (1) protect from danger and (2) provide pleasure and satisfaction. As we discussed earlier, traumatic situations place humans in danger and work against gaining pleasure. In a traumatic situation, human brains try to remove people from the dangerous setting or experience.

In *Culturally Responsive Teaching and the Brain* (2015) Zarretta Hammond presents a clear overview of the human brain and some of its functions. The complex architecture of people's brains develops in three layers, from the bottom up, like the floors of a house. Each layer is on top of the other, with the first layer being the oldest. These brain layers work both independently and in collaboration with one another in a coordinated manner. Let's take a look at the regions and functions of the brain and how each works to keep people safe.

The Reptilian Region

In *Brain-Based Learning* (2020), Eric Jensen outlines basic brain functions. This section provides a basic outline to help teachers of trauma-impacted students gain understanding of how the brain operations work and impact children.

At the base of the brain in its lowest level are the brainstem and cerebellum. This region is often referred to as the *reptilian region* because the structures here are similar to the brains of most reptiles (Jensen, 2020).

This brain region has limited thinking capacity and only reacts. Its major functions are protection and controlling automatic operations such as breathing, heart rate, blood pressure, and other actions that help keep people alive. Because the brain operates these automatic functions, it can also control them when people are in danger. This section of the brain also contains the medulla oblongata, which helps people constantly scan their environment for danger (Jensen, 2020).

In trauma-filled situations, the reptilian region of a child's brains reacts to the danger, bypassing the thinking and logical regions, and helping the child get out of the danger. This region of the brain helps children react quickly, often without thinking, to protect themselves (Jensen, 2020).

Students experiencing severe or multiple instances of trauma may come to rely on this reactionary behavior, and this reliance may spill over to the classroom. Since children's reptilian brain may be constantly scanning their environment for danger, small threats may trigger a reaction (Jensen, 2020). By working to implement a predictable, safe, and stable classroom environment, educators are trying to help children move their thinking to higher-level, more cognitive regions of the brain. This helps children become less reactionary. We'll talk about this concept in more detail later in the chapter.

The Limbic Region

Stacked directly on top of the reptilian region is the limbic region. It is also called "the emotional brain" (Hammond, 2015, p. 38). This emotional region is involved in processing emotional experiences. It helps people learn from past experiences and regulate emotions. While very complex operations occur in this region, there are three major functions processed here: (1) coordinating communication and information processing, (2) holding short- and long-term memory, and (3) controlling and communicating emotions, such as fear (Hammond, 2015). We'll examine this last region and some of its functions in more detail.

Hammond (2015) stresses the relationship between the *amygdala*, which is a component of the limbic region, and emotional processing. The amygdala sends a danger signal to the reptilian part of the brain using the hormone *cortisol*:

> We call this bypass an **amygdala hijack**. When the amygdala sounds its alarm with cortisol, all other cognitive functions such as learning, problem solving, or creative thinking stop. An amygdala hijack leads to our natural "fight, flight, freeze, or appease" responses. (Hammond, 2015, p. 40)

Since the brain is on auto pilot during perceived danger, these are reactions or responses, not cognitive strategies. When you know what's happening in students' brain when they are under stress, it can help explain you understand the emotional, seemingly irrational reactions you may encounter.

Brain Responses to Trauma

Humans have always had some exposure to stress and trauma. Throughout human history, there have been many physical dangers. People were exposed to attacks from wild animals, attacks from neighboring groups of people, danger within a social group or village, and a variety of other ever-present dangers originating in the natural and social worlds. If a wild animal was attacking someone, it was beneficial for that person to take one of three actions: (1) fight, (2) flight, or (3) hide. (We discuss this in more detail later in the chapter.) Human brains became accustomed to quickly making a determination of the best response and then communicating with the body to act out the decision. Making clear and quick decisions may have enabled people to survive.

As civilization changed over time and people organized themselves into more complex societies, threats from natural sources may have diminished. Fears stemming from older dangers may have been replaced by new threats. Think about the fears you hear about in the news and those expressed by your peers and friends. In analyzing several television commercials, we found threats such as home break-ins, social shunning by others, verbal altercations with neighbors, and road rage, among others. These and other fears can be very real and cause stress in the modern world. Contemporary dangers are often different than the dangers of the past, but your brain reacts to the angry shout of a driver cut off in traffic just as it might to the appearance of a saber-toothed tiger. In order to survive potentially big threats of the past, humans evolved to react dramatically to all threats—great or small. Educators we work with report that more and more families are under stress. This stress seemed to peak during the COVID-19 pandemic, which began in 2020.

Earlier, we discussed the work of Hammond (2015) and the outline of the typical danger response when the brain is under stress or attack. Fear activates a part of the brain called the *amygdala*. The amygdala stimulates the release of *cortisol*, which stops learning and stays in the body for two to three hours after the stressful event is over. The release of cortisol leads to a person's fight, flight, or hide survival behavior—whether that person is a soldier on the battlefield, an astronaut stepping onto the moon, or a student in his or her classroom. After a few hours, the body metabolizes the cortisol, and the person returns to a more normal state.

If a student experiences a stressful situation right before he or she leaves home for school, that stressful experience may stay with him or her for two to three hours. During this time, it may be difficult or impossible for the student to engage in learning. His or her brain may be still communicating that he or she needs to fight, run, or hide.

Shawn Nealy-Oparah and Tovi C. Scruggs-Hussein (2018) discuss two types of trauma: (1) *acute* (single event) and (2) *chronic* (continuous or multiple event). While both types affect the brain, their long-term impacts are very different. If a student experiences an acute or single traumatic event, his or her brain releases the cortisol, and the fight or flight response takes over. After the imminent danger or traumatic event passes, the student's brain returns to its normal state. Having dealt with the danger or traumatic event, the student may even develop improved coping mechanisms to address traumatic events in the future.

On the other hand, if a student is experiencing chronic ACEs simultaneously or several on a regular basis, he or she may be moving between the normal and arousal states repeatedly without the opportunity to remain in the normal, relaxed state. If the arousal state of the brain becomes the prevalent state because of multiple traumatic experiences or complex trauma, it can be hard for the brain to return to the normal, relaxed state (Nealy-Oparah & Scruggs-Hussein, 2018).

According to Hammond (2015), when children experience trauma, their brain may tell them to engage the fight, flight, hide, freeze, or appease response. Let's examine each of these five responses in more detail and how they can impact students in the classroom.

Fight

Using the fight response, a person stands his or her ground and fights back in traumatic situations. Children may have learned this approach. In fighting back, children are hoping they can remove the trauma by matching power for power. If a child is facing an intoxicated parent who becomes abusive, he or she may fight back to make the adult stop or see that the child will be a formidable match, causing the adult to back off or move away. Some children's personalities enable them to fight back right away, while others may need to have several traumatic episodes before building up to this response.

According to Jensen (2013), "Aggression enables a student to feel in control and take charge of a situation" (p. 17). Many trauma-impacted students don't have any level of control in their home lives. Their acts of aggression and acting out can be a way for them to gain some control over their lives.

Since the default response to match aggression with aggression may not be part of the child's normal behavior, a teacher may not see that a student has the capacity to strike out if a situation that triggers this behavior doesn't regularly occur in the school.

Flight

This behavior occurs when someone tries to get away or rapidly remove themselves from a traumatic situation. Flight behavior can occur when a child thinks he or she is weaker or subordinate to the person responsible for the traumatic situation. The flight can be a physical behavior or mental in nature. In a classroom, a student may actually get up and leave the learning situation. This flight may be the result of built-up stress from ongoing trauma.

Hide

When a person uses the hide behavior, he or she may try to avoid traumatic situations by disconnecting or trying to become invisible. The hide behavior is a way for children to withdraw and not be noticed during a traumatic event. John demonstrated the hide behavior whenever he dealt with his alcoholic parent. He would move away from the situation and hope nobody saw him. If his parent did find him, he would have to move to the flight or fight mode in order to deal with the situation.

In the classroom, children who have learned the hide behavior may seem to be daydreaming or withdrawn. They may not be able to answer questions when called on or easily connect with others. Confronting their behavior or calling them to attention will not make the situation better and may promote the hiding behavior instead.

Freeze

Closely related to hiding is the freeze behavior. People who exhibit the freeze behavior in traumatic situations may stop and be unable to move. Apparently, their brain doesn't know what action to take, so they can't take any action at all. Many of you have heard stories about people who are in the vicinity of a tragic incident but just froze. They couldn't leave or help the victim. After the traumatic incident passed, they wonder why they weren't able to act earlier.

Hopefully, you won't experience the freeze behavior in the classroom, but you may see effects of it. Similar to the hide behavior, children may daydream or *zone out* in response to a traumatic event, or they may not remember what happened in relation to an abusive situation. When you notice students excessively daydreaming, it may indicate something traumatic has happened to them. Providing an atmosphere where children feel safe and supported may be the best way to help them work through these experiences.

Appease

Children may have learned that the best way to respond to, or try to remove, a traumatic situation is to appease the person or persons inflicting the trauma. When children appease, they try to determine what the people in power are trying to gain and then give them what they want in the hope of making the situation go away. For example, if a child is dealing with an alcoholic parent who is drunk and aggressive, agreeing with that parent, doing what the parent is asking, and so on, can often decrease the parent's aggressive behavior.

In the classroom, you may see a child who constantly gives into others or lets others push him or her around. This can create situations in which some students dominate others. If this behavior continues over time, the child exhibiting appeasing behavior can become even more of a victim in the future.

How Personal Experiences With Trauma Can Shape Reactions

Because the prevalence of ACEs in the general population is so high, there's a good chance that many of you may have had your own experiences with ACEs. Having experienced childhood trauma may help you understand some of the situations your students are facing. In our own experiences, we try to have empathy for students experiencing trauma. On the other hand, we have also encountered trauma-impacted teachers who seemed less tolerant with some of their students who were experiencing trauma outside of school.

Since every situation and the reactions of each child is different (Nealy-Oparah & Scruggs-Hussein, 2018), teachers need to approach each traumatic situation based on the needs of the student. In part, this means that you should focus on the student's specific experience, not your own.

Let's see how Mr. Morris, an elementary school teacher, maintains his neutrality in working with students who experience trauma outside the school environment.

> *Mr. Morris, a fifth-grade teacher, works in a school where many children experience danger and trauma in their home neighborhood. Mr. Morris can understand some of their experiences since he also experienced trauma growing up, as his father was incarcerated and his mother addicted to drugs (two ACEs). Rather than make judgments or trying to pull personal information from his students, Mr. Morris works to establish a climate and routines that help students feel welcome and safe.*
>
> *One of his strategies is to allow students to move to a more private part of the classroom when they feel emotional or overwhelmed by something that happened to them at home. In the middle of learning activities, students can move to this area, no questions asked. If a student wants to talk about the situation later, he or she can make that choice; Mr. Morris doesn't force a conversation but has a process in place if a student wants to talk.*

In this scenario, Mr. Morris does not allow his own perspectives about overcoming a traumatic childhood environment to impact his actions with students. Mr. Morris has plenty of advice he could offer, but he knows students' situations could be different than his were and his guidance may not be appropriate. He offers empathy without dictating students' behavior and assuming that his students' experiences with trauma are like his own or that their forms of confronting their traumas should be like the ways he confronted his.

Throughout the rest of the book, we will provide more detailed descriptions of these focus areas and specific strategies for you to use in your classroom in order to implement the strategies that will best help trauma-impacted students.

Conclusion

In this chapter, we introduced concepts and research associated with childhood trauma, discussed how it impacts students, explored your own possible responses to trauma, and offered strategies to use in beginning to positively influence and respond to trauma-impacted students.

Let's revisit the scenario from the beginning of this chapter about Mr. Jackson and Thelma. Mr. Jackson started trying to understand Thelma and influence her reactions to the trauma she was experiencing outside the classroom.

> *Now that Mr. Jackson has gathered more information about how Thelma interacted in class before her parents' separation, he has a better understanding of what might be contributing to her lack of engagement. Because Thelma may feel let down by her parents due to the separation, Mr. Jackson thinks trust may be an issue. He examines his classroom to find situations that may be making Thelma less comfortable.*
>
> *He immediately notices that Thelma is seated on the far side of the classroom. She has to walk through the entire class to get to her seat. He also realizes that when he asks questions during discussions, he moves too quickly and isn't giving students a chance to think before calling on them for answers. Lastly, Mr. Jackson notices that he stands during many of his interactions with Thelma. The difference in height may be intimidating to her. He decides to refine his classroom practices to minimize these potentially uncomfortable situations and then tries to focus on Thelma's responses to see if he can detect more comfort on her part in the classroom.*

In this scenario, we are not trying to say that small, minor changes in classroom processes are going to completely eliminate the negative response to trauma at home that Thelma is still experiencing. However, Mr. Jackson is now aware of the situation and hasn't put Thelma on the spot and forced her to talk about it. He has made a few minor adjustments to help Thelma feel more comfortable and regain a sense of trust. In other student traumatic situations, it may be necessary to make more significant changes in the classroom, including involving the school counselor, psychologist, school principal, or others who could help provide more support and perspective.

In this chapter, you have learned more about what trauma is and can be and its potential impact on you and your students. This awareness helps you to gain an understanding and then use this understanding to focus on developing the appropriate attitude and mindset for effectively working with students of trauma.

In chapter 2 (page 31), we examine the importance of and the rationale behind a positive attitude and mindset when working with trauma-impacted students. You'll learn various strategies to avoid negative thought processes when encountering challenging students and situations to keep you on track.

QUESTIONS FOR *Reflection*

As you think about what you learned in this chapter and how it can be implemented in your classroom, reflect on the following questions.

- What is trauma? How do traumatic situations impact the brain?
- How is experiencing a single traumatic event different from experiencing complex trauma? Why are the aspects of complex trauma important for you to understand as an educator?
- How does understanding what happens in the brain during stress and conflict help you support a student who misbehaves? How might you use this information in your own classroom?
- How can your own experiences with trauma impact your work with students experiencing trauma?
- Why is trauma awareness important for you as an educator? How does improving your own awareness help you avoid possibly making traumatic situations worse for students?

chapter two

The Importance of Attitude and Mindset in Working With Trauma

Mr. Lynch is a high school teacher working in a school that serves a neighborhood where many students experience trauma and instability at home. There are times, especially after weekends or extended school breaks, when students' home experiences spill over and cause problems in his classroom. Mr. Lynch usually has to deal with most of these behaviors first thing in the morning during his homeroom period.

Mr. Lynch has learned to be prepared for these behaviors, not take them personally, and temper his reactions to maintain a sense of stability and calmness. He usually gets to school at least an hour before the students to get prepared for the day. As a part of his preparation, he checks to make sure the classroom is not crowded or cluttered. He makes sure he has his automatic check-in process ready and has needed student materials ready to go and easily accessible.

The final preparation Mr. Lynch does is mental. He thinks through the possible situations he may face and how he plans to address them. He turns on energizing music to help him gain a productive mindset and engages in productive self-talk to set his thoughts for success. He repeats to himself, "I get to do this" rather than "I have to do this."

Because he spends time preparing the environment and mentally preparing himself, he is ready to provide the attitude and environment the students need to help them connect with him and mentally move away from the traumatic situations they may be facing outside of school.

As you review this scenario, it may seem like Mr. Lynch is preparing for battle. In a way, he is. He's preparing for the battle of attitude, knowing that students are preparing to leave the traumatic situations they have been in outside of school and re-enter the supportive learning environment of their school and classrooms. Sometimes, this re-entry is bumpy and traumatic, so Mr. Lynch needs to prepare himself so he won't be consumed by negative thoughts or reactions as students re-enter the classroom presenting a variety of behaviors and attitudes.

In this chapter, we discuss the importance of and the rationale behind a positive mindset and attitude when working with trauma-impacted students. You'll also learn techniques and strategies to help you stay productive and avoid negative thoughts when encountering difficulties. As you review the information in this chapter, be sure to focus on the following.

- The power and importance of attitude and mindset when working with trauma-impacted students
- How to change traditional responses to behavior
- Strategies to stay calm and focused when dealing with students' emotional outbursts

These strategies will help you as you positively impact the success of all students, but especially those who may be trauma impacted.

The Power of Attitude and Mindset

In the groundbreaking book *Mindset: The New Psychology of Success*, Carol S. Dweck (2008) presents a strong case for the power of mindset. She states: "For twenty years, my research has shown the view you adopt for yourself profoundly affects the way you lead your life" (p. 6).

While most of Dweck's work cited in this book is focused on changing thinking and attaining goals, mindset also can influence how you approach situations. As noted in the following quote, other researchers present the case that mindset goes beyond goal setting and impacts how people approach almost everything in their lives. Daeun Park, Eli Tsukayama, Alisa Yu, and Angela L. Duckworth (2020) discuss the application of mindset beyond self-improvement:

> Recently, Duckworth (2016) proposed that a growth mindset might lead to grit. How so? Dweck (2017) argued that an individual's . . . belief about the

> malleability of personal attributes (e.g., mindset about ability and personality) can mold an individual's worldview, goals, and actions. Thus, in identical situations, differing beliefs about the world and ourselves profoundly influence how we react (Beck, Freeman, & Associates, 1990; Dweck, 2017). (p. 104889)

When people believe that their efforts will pay off, they are more likely to set long-term ambitious goals and persist to meet them. This idea of *grit* can help you develop the appropriate attitude and mindset to keep going and persevere when working with trauma-impacted students.

Develop Grit

There are two aspects in this quote related to our successful work with trauma-impacted students. First is the idea of grit. *Grit* refers to tenacity, sustained effort, and the ability to keep trying under adverse conditions. Working with trauma-impacted students can be challenging. It may be easy to give up or become discouraged. If you focus your mindset on being successful, you'll develop grit that will help you overcome situations that may seem to be impossible.

In the story at the beginning of this chapter, Mr. Lynch took the time each morning to focus and reflect on his mindset in working successfully with students. Let's see how this daily focus helps him to develop the grit he needs to tackle the situations he encounters with some of his students.

> *During his daily reflection, Mr. Lynch focuses on the general situations he may face but also thinks about one of his students, Omar. Each day, Omar enters the classroom, interacts very little with the other students, and goes directly to his seat and opens a book. When Mr. Lynch sees Omar enter the room, he makes it a point to welcome him. Omar doesn't respond but looks down and walks right past Mr. Lynch. Mr. Lynch suspects that Omar has difficulty developing trusting adult relationships as the result of some traumatic situation he is facing outside of school.*
>
> *The fact that Omar is so unresponsive is discouraging for Mr. Lynch. He wants to give up and just leave Omar alone. Whenever he has those thoughts, he has to engage in positive self-talk to keep persevering to build a relationship with Omar. If it takes all year, Mr. Lynch is going to keep trying to connect with Omar.*

In this brief example, Mr. Lynch uses positive self-talk to keep himself focused and optimistic in his relationship with Omar. Maybe someday, the work he has done to help Omar feel safe to connect will pay off. This is similar to the teacher who gives every student a cheery "good morning" regardless of the response he or she receives. If the objective is to *get* something, the motivation is entirely wrong. If the objective is to *give* something, to model the desired behavior, the motivation is consistent with promoting positive change in the student. It may take months before the student feels comfortable enough to return the greeting.

Getting a quiet student to talk may seem like a minor goal, but helping trauma-impacted students feel comfortable engaging in relationships with adults can be a major accomplishment. As we discuss later, it may be an adult in the student's life who is causing the trauma and breaking this level of trust.

Having grit as teachers is positive in many other more serious situations. Imagine a student who lashes out whenever he or she is slightly provoked. Having the ability to work to de-escalate this behavior requires mindset and grit to repeatedly keep working with the student. Grit helps you maintain a productive outlook and the belief that someday the interventions may start to moderate this behavior. Without a positive mindset and grit, it's much easier to give up and become discouraged.

Be Aware of Your Reactions

The second part of the quote by Park and her colleagues (2020) mentions the concept of *how we react*; reactions are crucial to success in working with trauma-impacted students. As we discuss later in the book, most of the traumatic situations students encounter involve some type of strong emotional experience. Because the students' emotions are heightened, they may not see (or learn) the value of calmness or of processing situations. Their normal world could include an adult who reacts violently to every situation. Since violent reactions are the norm, when teachers get upset, their reaction either reinforces students' trauma or is something they ignore since they see it all the time.

As the principal of a school serving a high number of trauma-impacted students, John noticed that when teachers scolded students for misbehaviors, many students just tuned them out. On the other hand, when students were treated calmly and asked to reflect on what they did, and how they planned to fix the problem they caused, many of these same students took the conversation to heart and started to make positive changes in their behavior. John and the teachers at this school observed that this approach was new to the students, and they couldn't just tune out the conversations. In a way, talking calmly and developing solutions was a mindset change for the students.

There are times when teachers need to react to situations in the classroom. If someone is in physical danger, stop the negative behavior immediately and prepare to react. In developing a trauma-impacted mindset, teachers must decide (based on the situation) when to react and when to remain calm. Without a trauma-informed mindset, some teachers just react every time no matter what the situation. Often these reactions make the situation worse that it was to start with for the teacher and the student.

In the work we do with teachers in trauma-impacted schools, an essential skill we teach is the ability to control reactions, whether positive or negative. The ability to step back, analyze the situation, then react in an appropriate manner is a key skill for working with trauma-impacted students.

Use Temporary Suspension of Opinion

In the book *Working With Difficult and Resistant Staff*, John F. Eller and Sheila A. Eller (2011) introduce a skill called *temporary suspension of opinion*. This skill is introduced as a way of working with adults to de-escalate emotions in tense situations. It also works well in situations with trauma-impacted students.

Temporary suspension of opinion is an internal skill that allows the receiver of communication (the listener) to withhold sharing an opinion about the message he or she heard from the sender. *Suspension* is used to increase the opportunity of thinking and problem solving on the part of the sender. Most people don't use suspension with much frequency, and normally experience the opposite of suspension. People are impatient with their thought process and give advice too quickly. This results in others finishing your sentences, prematurely giving their opinions, or not listening to the thoughts of others because they are busy formulating their own responses. When people use suspension, they are using it on a conscious level for a selected period of time for the purposes of truly listening, understanding another perspective, or to increase the problem-solving capacities of the sender.

Temporary suspension of opinion is a strategic skill that requires a lot of concentration on the part of the listener. It requires the listener to be very interested in listening to the sender of the message and understanding his or her perspective. Edgar H. Schein (2017), Massachusetts Institute of Technology professor emeritus, originally described this idea. The general idea of *suspension* means to set aside one's own reactions or impulses in order to understand what the other person is saying, or to truly listen to the other person.

In our work with teachers, we have found that there are three levels of temporary suspension of opinion that people experience. These are (1) listening level, (2) diagnostic level, and (3) emotional level.

1. **Listening level:** In the *listening level*, people find they are able to put their own need to talk on hold to listen more intently to the other person. Some people call this skill *active listening*. By listening to the other person more closely and intently, you'll find that you better understand what he or she is trying to say or communicate to you. Sometimes, by listening, you allow the other person to better understand his or her own problem or issue since he or she is able to describe it without being interrupted.
2. **Diagnostic level:** Once you have improved your ability to listen, the next level is called the *diagnostic level*. In this level, people are able to continue to listen intently to the message the other person is trying to communicate while simultaneously processing what their strategy should be once the person has communicated his or her thoughts. In some cases, as the listener, it would be better to ask a clarifying question. In other cases, it might be better to paraphrase or reflect back what you heard the other person say. All your reactions to the other person, once you've heard his or her initial message, will impact the next part of the communication.
3. **Emotional level:** The highest level of temporary suspension of opinion we encounter in our work is the *emotional level*. At the emotional level, the person listening steps back from the emotional aspects of the communication and remains objective. This level takes concentration and practice since it can be easy for some people to become emotional or emotionally involved in a situation.

> The emotional level is important because if your mind is overtaken by emotions, it's hard to think or cognitively process what's happening and generate solutions to the problem or issues. For example, if you get into a confrontation with a trauma-impacted student, and he or she says something like, "You don't care about me anyway." You might respond, "Yes, I do," and then you both begin to argue, getting deeper into the emotions and moving away from a solution. In the emotional level, you must learn how to remain sensitive to the situation, yet stay objective without getting taken hostage emotionally.

The skills of temporary suspension of opinion depend on your mindset or attitude in putting your own needs on hold to help trauma-impacted students be successful. These are outstanding skills for working with students, colleagues, family members, or anyone else you want to build a better relationship with over time.

Let's see how Mr. Lynch uses the skill of temporary suspension in working with one of his students.

> *On a Monday after a long holiday break, Mr. Lynch notices that one of his students, Brianna, is not focusing on the lesson he is teaching. Rather than upsetting her and addressing her behavior immediately in front of the class, he decides to wait until the students are in a discussion and then approach Brianna one to one. He walks over near Brianna's desk and asks her why she's not paying attention. Brianna gets angry and says, "Leave me alone; it's none of your business!" Mr. Lynch decides not to continue the confrontation, so he replies, "Let's talk for a few minutes at the end of class," and then slowly walks away. As he's walking away, Brianna continues to make comments and says she's not talking after class. Mr. Lynch refuses to continue the argument and walks away. Brianna gradually calms down.*
>
> *At the end of class, Mr. Lynch waits for some of the other students to leave and then approaches Brianna. He stays a few feet away so he is not in her personal space and says, "Brianna, I'd like to work together with you to come up with a plan to address what happened in class today so it doesn't happen again. When would be a good time for us to talk?" Brianna says, "Today is really bad for me. How about tomorrow morning?" Mr. Lynch agrees, and they set up a time to meet.*

In this scenario, Mr. Lynch stays calm during the initial confrontation but circles back to deal with it later when emotions are calmer. His goal is to work with Brianna to develop a plan to address the situation and try to avoid problems in the future, while not making her immediately conform in the classroom. Because he is able to step back and analyze the situation and Brianna's emotions, Mr. Lynch is able to keep the classroom confrontation from getting out of hand and exploding into an office visit or suspension. Brianna has spent a lot of time out of school or in the office in the past because of her behaviors. He knows the best place for her is in his classroom learning with her classmates.

Because temporary suspension of opinion is a conscious skill that you can choose to apply or not apply, if you need to react to a behavior right away, you can do that. If you decide to suspend for a few seconds, you can also do that. Temporary suspension of opinion allows you to provide a space between the action or behavior and your reaction to it. Sometimes, that space makes all the difference in working with trauma-impacted students.

Change Typical Reactions to Behaviors

Building on the skill of temporary suspension of opinion, another effective strategy to use in working with trauma-impacted students is to change the response they are accustomed to getting for their behaviors. Some students have learned to behave inappropriately to get a particular reaction from their teachers. In doing so, the students can almost predict the reactions they will get.

Let's see how this plays out in the following scenario.

> *Ms. Yung, a middle school Chinese immersion teacher, has one student, Gwen, who usually causes her problems in class. Gwen comes in late and doodles in her notebook. When Ms. Yung reminds Gwen that she needs to pay attention, Gwen becomes belligerent and asks Ms. Yung why she should pay attention. When Ms. Yung reminds her of the importance of paying attention, Gwen usually starts to argue with her. The argument usually gets out of control and ends up with Ms. Yung asking Gwen to leave the classroom and go to the office. As Gwen leaves the classroom, she shouts out a few obscenities and says, "Good, I didn't want to stay anyway!" This pattern of behavior is fairly frequent, happening at least once a week.*

In this scenario, Gwen is able to manipulate Ms. Yung into kicking her out of class on a regular basis. She can predict that Ms. Yung will get upset and react to her behavior by asking her to leave. This is one way for Gwen to gain control over a small part of her world. Gwen can control whether or not she has to stay in class. Let's see how Ms. Yung decides to address the situation.

Ms. Yung works with the school counselor to help her understand the situation with Gwen and how to change what is happening. The counselor suggests that Ms. Yung do the following.

- *Anticipate that Gwen could misbehave at any time and prepare for the behavior in advance.*
- *When Gwen does misbehave, use the skill of temporary suspension of opinion to step back and understand what's going on. Ms. Yung could also use this time to determine her next steps in working with Gwen.*
- *Try to move any confrontation outside of the classroom time or setting.*

After meeting with the school counselor, Ms. Yung feels she has a plan and the confidence to handle future incidents and disruptions from Gwen. She knows that above all else, she has to change her reaction of kicking Gwen out of class. She has to try to keep her in class.

To start the new process, Ms. Yung decides to meet with Gwen outside of class to try to change the dynamics of the relationship. During the meeting, Ms. Yung tells Gwen that she likes her and wants her to stay in class. She asks Gwen to share her perspective about the situation. Gwen tells Ms. Yung that she feels overwhelmed at times and just needs time alone. Ms. Yung and Gwen work out a signal for Gwen to let Ms. Yung know when she is feeling anxious. Ms. Yung sets up a quiet area for Gwen to go to when she feels the need. After two weeks, Gwen has not been sent out of the classroom. While there is still a lot of work to do, Gwen and Ms. Yung are on the right path to building a better relationship.

Changing your reaction to a behavior can have positive effects in the short term. Like Ms. Yung, teachers need to implement strategies to redirect the behaviors, work out plans with their students, or implement other strategies to change ingrained reactions. Schools that approach behavior with a trauma lens not only are getting better outcomes in school but also are helping build student resilience. So instead of asking, "What's wrong?" you may want to ask a question like, "What happened?" By asking a more open-ended question, you come across as less judgmental. You may also want to consider your knowledge of the student or what you know about him or her in asking supportive questions.

Even better, ask yourself what strengths students have as assets you can leverage so the focus is on the behavior and how students can change or replace the behavior with a more productive one. For example, if you know a student usually needs a few minutes to reflect before debriefing a situation, you'll want to wait before asking him or her to process. In this type of situation, you may want to start with more general prompts such as, "Please share your thought process in relation to . . ." or "As you think about what happened, what do you think started . . . ?" If you have a student who is very detail oriented, you may want to ask detail-related questions before prompting the student to draw conclusions. Helping students reflect on their situation may be less direct than just "getting to the point," but it might also be better in helping them understand and learn from the experience.

Accept Students for Who They Are

Another productive strategy related to attitude is to accept students for who they are. In accepting students, you look at them as assets rather than liabilities. In our work with colleagues, schools, and districts, it is increasingly apparent (and likely something we should have recognized at the outset of our careers) that the typical, average student does not exist. In fact, the sighting of one of these so-called typical students might rank with seeing Bigfoot or the Loch Ness monster. Instead of hoping for a classroom populated by mythical *normal* students, focus on the students you have and recognize the strengths they bring to your learning environment.

So, what might it take to become the teacher who accepts students for who they are—that unconditional teacher? This acceptance begins with letting go of the thoughts implied in the following comment from Jodi Wilgoren's (2000) *New York Times* article quoting Jim May, school superintendent in Escambia County, Florida: "When a low-performing child walks into a classroom, . . . instead of being seen as a challenge, or an opportunity for improvement, for the first time since I've been in education, teachers are seeing them as a liability." This notion of viewing some students as more work or demanding more time of teachers supposes a negative viewpoint that these students might not have redeeming qualities or be "salvageable." The reality is that oftentimes the students who challenge educators the most need them the most.

Unconditional teachers recognize that their own personal traits and characteristics might make it a challenge to like all students equally, and they commit to not playing favorites. More important, they find something interesting and appealing about each student. They use this insight to respond accordingly in times of struggle and in times of success. They have clear expectations in the classroom (expectations that students have helped to craft and in a language the students understand) while ensuring that students also know that their teacher's affection for every student and the support necessary for success does not need to be earned.

Evi Makri-Botsari (2001) suggests:

> Students who felt unconditionally accepted by their teachers were more likely to be interested in learning and to enjoy challenging academic tasks, instead of just doing schoolwork because they had to and preferring easier assignments at which they knew they would succeed. (p. 213)

Additionally, Alfie Kohn (2005) states:

> If some children matter more to us than others, then all children are valued only conditionally. Regardless of the criteria we happen to be using or the number of students who meet those criteria, every student gets the message that our acceptance is never a sure thing.

If teachers expect students to act in a particular way and tie their acceptance of and support for students in school to the desired behaviors, those teachers send a very clear message while also promoting concepts of artificial success and failure, in which these designations must be externally granted and based on subjective and sometimes arbitrary outside perspective. This often happens by well-intentioned adults who see themselves as trying to reinforce or eliminate specific student behaviors.

In the book *Learning to Trust*, Marilyn Watson (2003) suggests:

> If we want our students to trust that we care for them, then we need to display our affection without demanding that they behave or perform in certain ways in return. It's not that we don't want and expect certain behaviors; we do. But our concern or affection does not depend on it. (p. 30)

Having expectations, teaching those expectations, and reteaching those expectations when students stumble are all necessary ingredients for a positive classroom environment. Creating different tiers of student support and concern based on proficiency in those expectations is not.

Every year, teachers must establish classroom expectations, routines, predictable structures, and steps toward creating a learning community in which all students become proficient in the desired outcomes, including both behavior and academics. Clear classroom structure is beneficial to providing stable environments for children living in trauma. If your attitude in setting up your classroom is to provide a supportive, stable environment, students will benefit. If your goal in establishing expectations, routines, and rules is only to control students or make your own professional life better, the structure will not be beneficial. When teachers work toward accepting *all* students and the unique talents each student brings to school, the opportunities for achieving proficiency in the desired learning outcomes become more of a reality than a wish for every learner.

Although most teachers learn about Abraham H. Maslow's (1943) hierarchy of needs during teacher education, they can apply knowledge of these needs directly to working with trauma-impacted students. Maslow's *hierarchy of needs* is a motivational theory in psychology comprising a five-tier model of human needs, often depicted as hierarchical levels within a pyramid. From the bottom of the hierarchy upward, the needs are: physiological (food and clothing), safety (security), love and belonging needs (friendship), esteem, and self-actualization (Maslow, 1943).

Maslow's theory has made a major contribution to teaching and classroom management in schools. Rather than reducing behavior to a response in the environment, Maslow looks at the complete physical, emotional, social, and intellectual qualities of an individual and how they impact learning.

It's easy to see how Maslow's ideas find a place in the classroom. Before teachers can meet students' cognitive needs, they must first ensure students' physiological needs have been met. This has become more and more the responsibility of schools as greater awareness has led educators to take more demonstrable steps. For example, a tired and hungry student will find it difficult to focus on learning. Students need to feel emotionally and physically safe and accepted within the classroom to progress and reach their full potential.

Maslow's (1943) work also suggests that students should feel valued and respected in the classroom, so the teachers must create a supportive environment. Students with low self-esteem will not progress academically at an optimum rate until their self-esteem is strengthened.

As children develop, they must satisfy basic needs, especially those in the first three steps in Maslow's hierarchy: physiological, safety, and belonging. Students can't take the achievement step unless they have first taken the belonging step. In trauma-impacted situations, children may not get their most fundamental needs met. They cannot climb the next step in the hierarchy until they meet or attain the need in the previous step (Maslow, 1943).

If your goal is to help students be successful, you may need to go back and fulfill missing needs in your classroom. Building a predictable structure in the classroom may help fulfill students' need for safety. Once they feel a sense of predictability and safety, they can move forward to learn and grow academically.

A caring and effective classroom structure helps offer socio-emotional and academic support. As we note later in this book, trauma-impacted students may lack the basic needs essential for academic learning to occur.

Discover Students' DNA

To discover student strengths, teachers need to talk to their students and learn what skills, talents, character traits, and assets they bring to the classroom. This allows you to structure your lessons around these strengths and interests. One activity that supports this collection of student assets is to have students share their dreams, needs, and abilities—their *DNA*.

Provide students with a template that has the three letters, *D*, *N*, and *A*, written on it, and, after explaining what these letters stand for, invite them to list items corresponding to each letter. Encourage them to be authentic and not supply the answers they think adults might want to hear (for example, all students say their dream is to become a doctor); but instead, honestly share their thoughts and wishes. This provides teachers with great insight into each student, which they can use in building lessons. Teachers may want to share this information with other teachers in the building by posting a display board outside each classroom listing all students' information. Although this can be a very positive, affirming activity, always check with students first before posting any sensitive or personal information. Imagine the following example of a student's completed DNA template.

- **Dreams:** I want to learn everything I can about monster trucks and even how to drive them.
- **Needs:** I need help following directions and cleaning up.
- **Abilities:** I can make great art.

Would this information help you know your students better and plan for their year of learning? If this was posted outside your classroom door, would it help colleagues to know *all* students and not just *their* students?

In the simplest terms, an asset-based approach focuses on strengths you identify in all your students—and they *all* have strengths. Diversity in thought, culture, and traits are positive assets from which all students and adults can derive benefit. Members of the classroom community should be valued for what they bring to the classroom rather than defined by negative attributes. School can be a very stressful time for students. Sometimes they speak entirely different languages at home than they do in school, or maybe they have abilities that might be a departure from the perceived norm. Students from traumatic situations may see adult behaviors and aggression that others in their classroom don't see. The elements outside of the norm can result in students feeling peer pressure to behave and act in certain ways. For example, a student may have just experienced a traumatic event right before school but will need to put on a happy face so his or her peers and teachers don't see the pain.

Build on Gifts or Assets

Developing an asset mentality rather than a deficit mentality can change the entire outlook for both the teacher and student. Seeking to understand the unique gifts and talents each student brings to the learning environment helps build on these gifts.

Let's see how Mr. Garcia uses the asset mentality in his work with trauma-impacted students.

> *Mr. Garcia, a fifth-grade teacher, has three to four students in his classroom he suspects are living in traumatic conditions. These students regularly come to school in dirty clothes and smelling like smoke. They keep to themselves and don't seem to be making a lot of friends in the classroom. Rather than judging them and writing*

them off as unimportant, poor performers, or troubled, Mr. Garcia decides to reach out and build relationships with them.

After a week of making an effort getting to know the students, Mr. Garcia starts to notice the unique strengths each of them possesses. Amanda seems very organized; Billy seems to have very creative thoughts and ideas; and Tammy is very conscientious in completing her work and projects. Mr. Garcia decides that rather than focus on their problems (he still keeps their potential traumatic situations in the back of his mind), he will focus on their strengths. Since Amanda, Billy, and Tammy get dropped off at school much earlier than the other students, Mr. Garcia decides to give each of them a classroom job. The students seem surprised Mr. Garcia wants them to help, but all say yes to his offer.

Each morning, when they come to class, Amanda, Billy, and Tammy all get right to work. They take care of the tasks Mr. Garcia gives them and ask for more things to do. After a couple of weeks, some of the other children notice they are working and start to talk with them. Soon, Mr. Garcia notices that Amanda, Billy, and Tammy are more comfortable in their conversations with their classmates. It seems that all three are starting to make friends with their peers.

In this scenario, Mr. Garcia's efforts to see the positive aspects of these three students helps them feel more comfortable and contribute to the classroom. Focusing on their strengths helps them move beyond the challenges they face outside of school.

John had a similar experience when he was in middle school. Because of the trauma of his home environment, he was shy and not very outgoing. One of John's teachers asked him to come in early to help with some classroom projects. This gesture made John feel valued and important. Due to increased feelings of confidence, John started to get more involved in other aspects of school, including sports. Participating in sports helped distract John from the trauma he faced at home, feel more confident in working with others, and provided a focus for him to work hard and improve his life.

As a teacher, you are significant to the students you teach. An action that may seem minor to you may be very important to one of your students. Looking for and accessing the unique talents and strengths of your students can have very positive effects and may even change a life.

Calmness and Stability

Because many of the traumatic situations students face are not calm and stable, students are accustomed to being in a state of chaos. This constant state of chaos is not only taxing to the brain but also can be harmful to processing and learning. In your classroom, establishing and maintaining a steady calm state is very important. Here, we discuss the importance of mindset in providing a foundation for calmness and stability.

Most human actions are grounded in thoughts. If you set your mind to being calm and tempering your reactions, eventually, you'll be able to control how you react to situations, even those that seem to be unpredictable. We refer to the ability to control reactions as *unflappability*. If you are unflappable, you don't let things get to you, get under your skin, or make you upset. You roll with the punches and are ready for almost anything.

Some of the very best teachers exhibit this ability, but it goes hand in hand with being alert and aware of what is going on in the classroom at all times. This ability is so important to teacher success that Robert J. Marzano (2017) includes it in his model of effective instruction. He calls this behavior *withitness*. In exhibiting withitness, teachers are able to scan the entire classroom, monitor situations and de-escalate them before they get out of control, be proactive, and implement other calming behaviors.

In *Fostering Resilient Learners,* Souers and Hall (2016) identify a concept a teacher called "the sea of forgetfulness" (p. 52). The *sea of forgetfulness* is the process of addressing a student misbehavior and then allowing that student to leave the incident behind and start over. We have advocated a similar concept called *clean slate*. In the practice of clean slate, students are able to deal with a classroom problem and then start fresh each day. We have found great success in implementing processes like the sea of forgetfulness or clean slate.

There are several simple tools that can help you in keeping calm and setting a stable, supportive classroom environment. You may have used these tools in the past in other settings. You'll find them extremely valuable as you use them for developing calm, supportive learning environments.

Apply Temporary Suspension of Opinion

We discussed this strategy earlier in the chapter with regard to developing greater support for students in part by helping the students keep calm; you can also use this skill to help you remain calm while reducing your propensity to judge. You can use each of the three levels of suspension (listening, diagnosic, and emotional).

Paraphrase and Reflect

The skills of paraphrasing and reflecting help you try to clearly understand the message the other person is sending. As a teacher, it's crucial to make sure you understand what your students are trying to tell you. Educators all have made the mistake of assuming they know what students are telling them and moving forward only to find out they are addressing the wrong problem.

One way to avoid reacting and communicate that you are listening is to rephrase or *reflect* to the student what you think you heard before moving forward. This understanding check is best accomplished using paraphrasing and reflecting. In addition to helping you understand what students are telling you, it also can serve as a way of calming down situations. We have used this skill to calm down many emotional conversations.

Paraphrasing is a skill you may have been introduced to in your teacher preparation program or early in your teaching career. *Paraphrasing* is the process in which the receiver of the message restates the message to ensure the receiver heard its intent. In paraphrasing, the statement made by the receiver is somewhat indirect. For example, a person receiving a message might say, "I want to make sure I understand what you said. I think I hear you saying that you are upset about the situation?" Paraphrasing statements helps provide an opportunity for the receiver to get clarification before a lack of understanding leads to frustration.

Reflecting statements are similar to paraphrasing statements except reflections are more direct. A reflecting statement based on the situation in the previous paragraph might sound like this: "You're upset about the situation." This statement is checking to make sure the message from the sender is understood, but the reflecting statement is more direct in nature.

In addition to improving your ability to listen, paraphrasing and reflecting helps you to be less judgmental with students. When you take the time to pause the conversation and seek clarity, it's much harder to judge and draw conclusions. By using paraphrasing and reflecting, you seek to understand the other person and not draw conclusions. This momentary pause for clarity communicates to the other person that you are interested in learning more. These two strategies are effective for trauma-impacted students because they allow you as a listener to truly listen and understand.

Let's see how Mr. Lynch, the teacher in a scenario earlier in the chapter, uses paraphrasing and reflecting to avoid judgment in working with one of his students.

> *As Mr. Lynch prepares for the start of class, one of his students, Dakota, comes in. Dakota seems angry and upset, making a lot of noise and talking to himself as he puts his supplies and books in his desk. Mr. Lynch slowly walks over to Dakota. He has learned in past interactions with Dakota not to make sudden movements or appear confrontational. Mr. Lynch asks, "How are you doing, Dakota?"*
>
> *Dakota replies, "Terrible, it was a bad morning."*
>
> *"It sounds like things didn't go well this morning."*
>
> *Dakota responds, "No, they didn't. My mom overslept because she was out late last night. We had to rush around to get ready."*
>
> *Mr. Lynch says, "I can tell that was upsetting."*
>
> *"Yes, I'm glad you understand."*
>
> *Then Mr. Lynch asks, "Would you like to talk about it so we can work together to make this a great day?"*
>
> *"Yes."*
>
> *"Where would you like to start?" Mr. Lynch asks.*

In this brief scenario, Mr. Lynch takes the time to let Dakota know he is listening. In the entire conversation, Mr. Lynch does not offer a solution until the end. He does this after Dakota tells him he thought he understood the situation. Dakota then accepts an invitation from Mr. Lynch to talk but only after he knows Mr. Lynch is interested in helping and not judging. Paraphrasing and reflecting convey the desire to listen and understand before judging. They are powerful tools to use when working with trauma-impacted students.

Ask Open-Ended Questions

Another power tool to use in working with trauma-impacted students is open-ended questioning. While paraphrasing and reflecting help teachers better understand what a student has just told them, open-ended questioning helps teachers to work with the student by probing into the details around the situation.

A key to the success of probing is the focus on asking open-ended, nonjudgmental questions. Asking a question like, "What were you thinking during the incident?" is less judgmental than "Why did you do that?" which seems to convey judgment. The open-endedness of the question allows the student to share what he or she is comfortable sharing by talking through the details. In the scenario, Mr. Lynch asks Dakota, "Where would you like to start?" Mr. Lynch knows Dakota is ready to talk about the situation when Dakota says *yes* to his lead-up question, "Would you like to talk about it so we can work together to make this a great day?" The answer to that question gives Mr. Lynch the opening and permission to probe more deeply with Dakota.

In addition to gaining more information about Dakota and his thoughts, asking open-ended questions helps Mr. Lynch stay calm and lower the potentially emotional situation. From our experience, opening up the possibility of more than one answer promotes a conversation rather than a confrontation.

Use a Combination of Strategies

The skills of temporary suspension of opinion, paraphrasing and reflecting, and open-ended questioning work well on their own, but their power is multiplied when used together strategically. When teachers try to use the skills simultaneously, there can be a short learning curve at first, but with continued support and practice, these skills become second nature. When we work with teachers of trauma-impacted students, we have them practice combining these skills so they become proficient and comfortable. As you become comfortable with each skill individually, consider combining two or three of them together and watch how your confidence and skill level grows.

Conclusion

In this chapter, we focused on the importance of attitude and how it impacts your work with trauma-impacted students. First, we discussed the value of mindset and how it can determine both how teachers approach situations and how they react to those situations. Monitoring both your approach and reactions are important if you are going to be successful in your work with trauma-impacted students.

We also examined the power of accepting students for who they are and understanding their DNA (dreams, needs, and abilities) in helping them be successful in and out of the classroom. Finally, we looked at three skills (temporary suspension of opinion, paraphrasing and reflecting, and open-ended questioning) that can help you effectively communicate with students while minimizing your judgment. These skills help teachers truly seek to understand students rather than trying to fix them or guide them toward a prescribed solution to a problem or situation.

Your attitude is closely connected with your success in working with trauma-impacted students. As you approach challenging situations, keep this important aspect in mind. Thinking about attitude will increase your success and help your students build positive connections with you.

In chapter 3, we take a closer look at the foundational elements that must be in place to help you transform your classroom into a trauma-informed and sensitive place where all students, not just those suffering from trauma, can shine.

QUESTIONS FOR *Reflection*

As you think about what you learned in this chapter and how it can be implemented in your classroom, reflect on the following questions.

- Why is attitude so important in successfully working with trauma-impacted students? How can your attitude help you approach and work with the situations you may encounter in your classroom?
- How can temporary suspension of opinion help you avoid reacting to the situations you encounter? What are the various stages of temporary suspension of opinion, and how is each stage important in your work with trauma-impacted students?
- How does accepting students for who they are affect your success in working with students?
- What are the attributes of student DNA, and why are they important?

chapter three

Classroom Structures to Support Trauma-Sensitive Practices

In Ms. Montoya's fourth-grade classroom, the climate is calm and accepting. When students enter the room, Ms. Montoya has processes in place for them to check in and reflect on their learning mood. As a part of this check-in procedure, students use their nameplates to identify one of the three following moods.

- *Ready to learn*
- *Need a few minutes to reflect on my learning mood*
- *Need to talk to my teacher*

Ms. Montoya knows that several of her students come from traumatic situations and environments, and she has taught them how to reflect on their learning mood and feel comfortable in letting her know their mood so she can help them address their mood and get ready for learning. She watches the check-in board to note students who don't place their nameplates in the "ready to learn" category. She either reaches out to them before the class meeting first thing in the morning or monitors their interactions throughout the day to make sure she is ready if they need support.

The check-in process is one of many foundational practices that Ms. Montoya incorporates into her classroom to help provide a welcoming and predictable environment to her students. Since she learned the importance of developing a positive and supportive learning environment and has constructed one that is stable and predictable, she has noticed a real difference in student behavior. The morning check-in is just one of the many procedures Ms. Montoya incorporated into her teaching to help make her classroom more trauma sensitive.

In this chapter, you'll learn the importance of providing a predictable and stable learning environment for trauma-impacted students. You'll also learn how this stable and predictable environment can be beneficial to *all* students, including those who do not experience multiple or complex trauma outside of school.

As you review the information in this chapter, be sure to focus on the following.

- The role that stable and predictable environments have in helping children's brains cope with trauma and move back into learning modes
- Ideas and strategies to help develop stable and predictable learning environments
- Methods for responding to trauma behaviors in the classroom
- How to establish a trauma-sensitive classroom environment

While establishing and implementing a predictable and stable classroom environment won't fix every trauma-related problem, it will go a long way in helping improve learning for *all* students, not just those impacted by trauma.

The Trauma-Sensitive Classroom

In chapter 1 (page 13), we discussed information related to brain operations and stress. Specifically, Jensen (2020) and Hammond (2015) discuss the impact of cortisol on the brain. When cortisol is present, the thinking parts of the brain are suspended or on hold. This is one reason why people under stress or in conflict may seem to be irrational. They may do things that don't make sense. Their brains cannot move to a cognitive or thinking mode until the cortisol level has decreased, enabling rational thought and processing. According to Hammond (2015), "Cortisol stops all learning in the body for about 20 minutes and stays in the body for up to 3 hours" (p. 76).

Students experiencing trauma at home may come to school with significant levels of cortisol in their brains or systems. Even though teachers haven't necessarily been the cause of student trauma or stress, they can be the recipient of students' misbehavior. If it can take up to three hours for the body to metabolize cortisol (Hammond, 2015), it makes sense that teachers should try to reduce or minimize stressful situations and environments to allow this metabolizing process to take place. Providing a calm, predictable classroom structure and environment is one way to reduce stress. In the following scenario, let's see how Ms. Montoya uses a strategy to assess her students' readiness to learn and then tries to help one of her students, Polly, avoid a situation that could elevate her emotions and stress.

> *As students use the check-in system that asks about their readiness to learn, Ms. Montoya notices that Polly has stood at the board for a minute or two deciding how to rate her learning readiness. Ms. Montoya waits and sees that Polly has rated herself as "Need a few minutes to reflect on my learning mood." She knows from her past experiences with Polly that she could be in a stressful state. Ms. Montoya also knows that Polly will need a few minutes to relax and get herself under control before interacting with her classmates.*
>
> *Ms. Montoya sees two other girls starting to approach Polly. She knows this may lead to a negative reaction from Polly, so she intervenes by asking the girls to help with a classroom job. They come right over and leave Polly alone. Once Ms. Montoya has started the girls on the job, she approaches Polly. When she is still a few feet away, she gently welcomes Polly and tells her it's OK to take a few minutes to reflect. She gestures toward a beanbag chair in the corner where Polly can sit. Ms. Montoya monitors the situation from afar, making sure no other students bother Polly. After about ten minutes, she notices that Polly gets up from the beanbag chair and joins in on some of the activities Ms. Montoya planned to keep students busy while they are getting ready for the opening of the day and the classroom morning meeting.*

By monitoring students' check-in status, Ms. Montoya avoids a possible problem. She redirects the girls before an altercation with Polly can occur. Ms. Montoya gives Polly the space she needs to move beyond an earlier possible traumatic event to get into a more cognitive mindset. Because Ms. Montoya understands the possible impacts of trauma on the brain, she knows Polly has to allow any possible cortisol to be metabolized from her brain so she can move out of the arousal state.

Classroom Structures and Procedures

Effective teachers periodically examine both the structure and procedures they use in their classrooms to ensure that the environment is trauma sensitive. A trauma-sensitive learning environment is one designed by the teacher to minimize its impact on continuing or extending traumatic situations for students. Examining your classroom to ensure it is trauma sensitive can be complex at first but will be easier as you get to know your students.

When determining ways to sensitize your classroom, try to put yourself in students' shoes. If the procedure or process you have in mind is not essential to the safe operation of your school, it may be a candidate for closer examination. If you notice that a certain procedure or process triggers an undesirable student reaction or behavior, it may be a candidate for review and possible elimination. Operating your classroom using predictable, essential procedures can help eliminate unnecessary disruption and issues for students. Teachers we have worked with report that they find benefits in having students involved in setting up some of the classroom rules and procedures.

Let's see how providing student involvement and allowing them some sense of control in setting up classroom procedures works in Mrs. Jennings's classroom in the following scenario.

> *Mrs. Jennings, a high school teacher, knows that many of her students go home to a dangerous neighborhood each afternoon. Mrs. Jennings has heard that tense situations can develop suddenly in this neighborhood without warning or notice, and this results in some students not knowing if something bad is about to happen when they get home. The events of the neighborhood are outside of these students' scope of control.*
>
> *Mrs. Jennings has worked to make her classroom routines very predictable and logical. She uses consistent processes for students to receive and turn in completed assignments. She involves her students in helping to establish classroom rules. She provides choices for students, so they can feel a sense of control and learn decision-making skills. She watches her students carefully so she can pick up possible triggers that might set off behavior problems. She speaks in a very calm and soft voice.*

In this scenario, Mrs. Jennings modifies some of her processes to provide stability for students that they may not have when they go home to their neighborhood. Since they spend many more hours outside the classroom than in it, it may take students considerable time to become accustomed to her trauma-sensitive classroom and believe it's a dependably safe environment. Mrs. Jennings constantly monitors situations to head off potential problems.

All teachers should consider completing an assessment of their learning environment, looking for areas that might be contributing to trauma or adding to outside traumatic situations. The template in figure 3.1 (page 56) can help you identify potential problem areas and make necessary adjustments to make your classroom learning environment more trauma sensitive.

In their article, "Trauma-Informed Leadership in Schools: From the Inside-Out," Nealy-Oparah and Scruggs-Hussein (2018) identify what they call the *eight Rs* or areas of focus for schools and classrooms to become more trauma sensitive. The first four Rs are focused on teacher behaviors and attitudes. They are all related to teacher responses.

- **Realize:** Trying to understand the situations some students are experiencing
- **Recognize:** Being observant so you can see the signs of trauma and the triggers of student responses to trauma
- **Respond:** Responding in a productive manner to students' reactions to impacts of trauma
- **Resist:** Resisting judgmental responses to trauma-related student behavior

The second four Rs are focused on classroom practices and structures that can help mediate the impacts or responses to trauma.

- **Routines:** Having friendly and consistent processes in place for learning, management, and student behavior
- **Rituals:** Designing processes, ceremonies, and celebrations to help students feel valued and special
- **Relationships:** Developing and nurturing positive relationships with students in the school and classroom
- **Regulation:** Providing processes and strategies to help students productively cope with, de-escalate, or let go of the emotions associated with the trauma or traumatic situations they are experiencing so these emotions don't negatively impact learning

List the suspected trauma areas that may be impacting your students. __________ __________ __________ __________
List the processes or procedures in your learning environment that seem to trigger undesirable behaviors. __________ __________ __________ __________
List the evidence that makes you think these processes or procedures are triggering problems. __________ __________ __________ __________
Implement changes in processes or procedures that you think would help make your learning environment more trauma sensitive. __________ __________ __________ __________
What is your timeline for making these changes in your classroom? What resources will you need in order to make these changes? __________ __________ __________ __________

Figure 3.1: Template for identifying and changing potential learning environment problem areas.

Visit ***go.SolutionTree.com/behavior*** *for a free reproducible version of this figure.*

Classroom Considerations in Response to Trauma Behaviors

While children may experience similar incidents of trauma (for example, neglect, abuse, and exposure to drug addiction), their reactions might be quite different. Two of your students may be experiencing verbal abuse at home, but one may be on edge and strike out when the slightest issue arises (fight response). The other may be withdrawn and seek to avoid contact (hide or appease). The reaction of any of your trauma-impacted students could be unpredictable.

While it's important for you to respond in a personal way to each student, there are some foundational classroom structures that help trauma-impacted students feel support and a sense of trust, and also help increase their ability to learn in the classroom.

Teacher Attitude and Demeanor

In order to help all students be successful, especially students facing trauma, you must have a good attitude and a caring demeanor. Since educators teach children first and content second, the teacher's attitude is critically important. Students living in traumatic homes and experiencing emotional situations need unconditional support.

From 2000–2008, John worked with teachers to develop their teacher leadership and action research skills. During this work, he conducted an activity in which he gave the participants a grid containing thirteen spaces. He asked group members to write in a significant memory from each of their thirteen (including kindergarten) years of primary and secondary educational experiences. In all the groups, nobody identified content as his or her most significant memory. All these educators identified emotional connections they made with their teachers. The emotional connections and support are the most significant experiences students have with their teachers.

Like those teachers, John (growing up in a single-parent, trauma-filled home) also has significant memories of teachers who looked beyond the impact of his home life to see what was good and strong within him. They were able to teach John not just social studies, science, mathematics, or physical education, but also helped him feel welcomed and loved. His experiences of emotional connection with his teachers helped shape John and how he planned to break the cycle of trauma with his own family. The attitude and demeanor of his teachers helped to overcome the emotional injury caused by the trauma.

Think about why you decided to become a teacher and what gifts you bring to make a positive impact on students' lives. In *Thriving as a New Teacher*, Eller and Eller (2016) offer several templates to help teachers reflect on their purpose and strengths. You can visit www.solutiontree.com/free-resources/instruction/tnt to find these templates online.

Classroom Culture

In *Seven Keys to a Positive Learning Environment in Your Classroom*, Tom Hierck (2017) discusses the importance of classroom culture in determining student success: "When seeking to develop a successful, supported collaborative learning community, teachers must first develop a positive classroom culture" (p. 9).

Consider classroom culture as the way educators do business, embracing the common ideas that hold them together and the bottom line in how they work together as a learning community to help ensure everyone is successful. In classrooms that have strong, supportive cultures, students work together toward common goals; they listen to and respect each other. When an incident occurs, students work together to address it so they can get back to their normal collaborative, caring culture.

Even though both students and teachers live the culture of supportive, collaborative classrooms and schools, it's teachers who help establish, nurture, and strengthen this culture. Let's see how Ms. Montoya establishes and strengthens the culture in her classroom.

> *As Ms. Montoya prepares for the upcoming school year, she knows it will be important for her fourth-grade students to help establish the expectations and structures in their classroom. She designs an activity to let them share their thoughts about what they feel they need in their learning environment to feel safe and learn. The end product of this conversation is a classroom covenant of expectations for students and Ms. Montoya to follow to make the classroom a productive place for everyone. In developing the covenant, Ms. Montoya suggests the entire class revisit it and examine how it was working during their normal morning meetings.*

While Ms. Montoya reminds students when behaviors are deviating from the covenant, after a few weeks, she decides it's time for the group to discuss the topic and develop strategies to refocus their efforts. As Ms. Montoya helps guide the discussion, she reminds students of their discussion norms and to be sure to listen to everyone before making a decision.

The students decide that they will remind each other when they are not following the guidelines in the covenant. These reminders will be positive and supportive, reflecting their classroom culture. After their agreement, classroom behaviors are more in line with the expectations they developed in their classroom covenant. When problems arise, they work together to address them.

The way Ms. Montoya handles her classroom expectations with students is aligned with the classroom culture she helps her students develop. Since one aspect of the culture is shared responsibility, it makes sense for Ms. Montoya to involve students in solving behavior issues rather than generating the solutions herself. Her style of intervention matches the classroom culture she nurtures. Establishing and nurturing a caring and collaborative classroom culture also helps develop trust between her and her students. The students trust that Ms. Montoya will address situations in a respectful manner based on the culture they have established. They also trust that she will discuss with them any issues taking place in relation to classroom expectations. By being consistent in her approach, Ms. Montoya is able to build this high level of trust.

A Sense of Caring and Relationship

While it would be difficult to have the same relationship with every student, developing some sort of relationship in which students know their teachers care and are looking out for them is essential.

In *Fostering Resilient Learners*, Souers and Hall (2016) describe the difficulty of maintaining relationships with students who have or are experiencing trauma: "Relationships are not easy. . . . Just managing 'normal' relationships with our friends, coworkers, and family can be challenging. When we bring trauma-affected students into the equation, the delicate nature of relationships stands out even more clearly" (p. 90).

Students experiencing trauma may resist developing relationships with adults because of the lack of trust they may have in the adults who have caused or contributed to the trauma in their lives. Nealy-Oparah and Scruggs-Hussein (2018) state:

> This is a key reason that many students have trouble being able to trust adults, as the adults in their lives may be causing "vicarious trauma"—trauma being experienced from someone in the family, such as a parent who is suffering from illness, mental health conditions or being abusive—all causing wounds for the student who continues to be injured through re-traumatization and is not given time to heal. The adults closest to them are not providing security; thus trusting a "safe adult" is not a reality or comfortable. (p. 13)

From this research, you can see why children have such difficulty in trusting any adults if the trauma is caused by a close adult. Keep this in mind so you can understand if you encounter resistance in trying to build a trusting relationship with a student who has experienced trauma.

Your relationship with each student may be different and that's OK. The important thing is that you are aware of this need and take steps to develop relationships with all students. This explains why some students become more withdrawn or even strike out more when teachers reach out to help them.

Predictable Structures

One characteristic of the traumatic situations some students face is unpredictability. Students may not know when the drunk or drug-addicted parent, boyfriend, or other family member may come home and want to beat up on them physically or emotionally. They may be neglected in one instance and taken care of in another. The random nature of their lives can keep the defensive mechanisms of their brains on high alert all the time.

It's crucial that your classroom be a place of emotional predictability and consistency in its operation. From our own classroom experiences and comments from teachers we work with, the stability of the environment helps trauma-impacted students let their guard down and focus on their learning.

Developing check-in procedures, having consistent strategies for dealing with issues, and operating a predictable schedule help *all* students, including those impacted by trauma, focus on learning. The procedures need to match the needs of the learners and your own needs as a teacher. Figure 3.2 provides a template to help teachers plan their classroom arrangement to meet students' needs and accommodate their preferred teaching style.

Directions: Respond to the following questions to help you determine the optimal arrangement for your teaching style and your students' needs. Once you have reflected on the questions, draw a map of your classroom arrangement.
1. What kinds of instructional strategies do you plan to use in your classroom? Write the percentage you think you use each strategy during a typical week. Using the information from this exercise, select the classroom arrangement that will best accommodate the most common instructional strategies you use in your classroom. __________ Lecture, presentation __________ Small-group work, discussion, debates __________ Individual work and projects __________ Short presentations followed by note taking __________ Large-group presentation followed by work on a device (notebook or tablet, and so on) __________ Other
2. How well behaved are your students? What kinds of issues do you encounter with them during instruction and individual or group-work time? This aspect may be hard for you to determine definitively as a new teacher. You may get some ideas from your initial interactions with students before school starts or through conversations with your colleagues or mentor. If you have no idea what student behavior might be like, select classroom arrangements that will minimize interactions to start the year (for example, presenter).
3. Draw a map of your potential room arrangement.
4. Review your potential room arrangement. What issues might you encounter if you implement this arrangement? How could you prevent or overcome these issues to help make your arrangement a success?

Source: Eller & Eller, 2016, p. 38.

Figure 3.2: Planning your classroom arrangement.

Visit ***go.SolutionTree.com/behavior*** *for a free reproducible version of this figure.*

Movement

As discussed earlier in this chapter, trauma impacts the brain in ways that are good for survival but not always good for learning. When students experience repeated or multiple types of trauma, the introduction of flight or fight hormones (cortisol) can move brain functions from cognitive to reactionary. When the brain is either in an arousal state or repeatedly experiences arousal because of trauma, it may be difficult for students to sit for long periods of time without movement. It is difficult for all students, not just students dealing with trauma.

Offering periodic and scheduled movement opportunities allows students to burn off steam and stay focused. Incorporating movement into lessons at regular intervals helps to re-energize learning channels in the brain plus reduce boredom. You may have noticed that even a thirty-second stand-up-and-stretch break can work miracles in re-energizing students' attention spans.

Some who teach at the secondary level may think the passing time between classes provides all the movement students need. While walking from class to class does energize students, it's not enough to help them burn off negative energy and anxiety and regain their focus on learning.

A good rule of thumb is to think about students' need for movement from your own perspective. How long could you sit in a professional development session or meeting without movement before you started to feel anxious? How much time would you like to see between movement opportunities?

While there are many ways to incorporate movement into your classroom, we've found those that are the least detailed or complicated seem to make the most sense. These include the following.

- Standing up periodically to stretch
- Meeting with another classmate to discuss an aspect of the lesson
- Partway through the lesson, having students meet in small groups
- Asking students to show their learning by holding up their papers, signaling with their hands, pointing, or other simple movements
- Asking students to vote on answers by moving to different parts of the room
- Taking a one-minute walk as a group around the classroom
- Using manipulatives in learning

The strategies you choose to implement should match your teaching style (and personal comfort requirements) and students' needs, and fit the culture of your classroom. If you keep these aspects in mind, the movement will seem like a natural part of your instruction rather than something out of the blue that will confuse or even cause disruptions.

Reflection or Metacognition

Through our experiences in the classroom, one of the most effective management strategies to help students understand their own behaviors is to allow them to process their thoughts and actions. You may know this skill as reflection or metacognition. It is especially helpful for trauma-impacted students because some of their life may be irrational and out of control. They don't see reflective behaviors modeled or encouraged by the people who cause them trauma, nor do they see their traumatic situations as ones in which reflection is valued. Students may move from one traumatic situation to another. Because of the constant or multiple traumatic situations many of them face, they may never get a chance to reflect on their own actions in these traumatic events.

In *Fostering Resilient Learners*, Souers and Hall (2016) emphasize that reflection can help trauma-impacted students think about where they are in their own emotional response to trauma. These authors share a story about their work with one student. In this story, they ask the student to reflect on where he is in his thinking, either using the *upstairs* part of his brain (thinking and problem solving) or the *downstairs* (reactionary and defensive). The activity helps this student know his mind state so he can move toward resolution of the situation. By offering students opportunities to reflect several times each day, teachers help them monitor their own state of mind so they can gradually gain control of their emotions.

In the scenario at the beginning of the chapter, Ms. Montoya uses a check-in process in which she asks students to think about, then report their state of mind at the beginning of the school day. Trauma-informed teachers use a variety of techniques to help students reflect on and report their state of mind during the day, such as following.

- Asking students to write down their thoughts for a few minutes and then read their writings
- Developing an *emotion meter* students keep on top of their desks; during reflection time, students use markers or some other means to rate their emotions
- Having laminated green, yellow, and red cards (like the ones used by sports referees) students can display to show their moods or emotions. When students display a yellow card, the teacher knows to check in

with the student to see what he or she needs to move back to the green card. If a student shares a red card, the teacher knows the student may need immediate attention or should move to a quiet location to get his or her emotions back in control.

- Offering midday classroom meetings (similar to morning meetings) that allow students to discuss and process happenings in the classroom that may be impacting their emotions

You are only limited by your creativity in developing strategies to help students reflect on and take control of their emotions. Being able to manage emotions is one element of building resilience that trauma-impacted students need in order to keep themselves on track and avoid allowing situations to trigger their negative emotions.

Let's look at how Ms. Montoya uses predictable structures in her classroom to help students be successful.

> *In her fourth-grade classroom, Ms. Montoya develops a clear and predictable schedule for each day. Certain rituals (like morning meetings) occur every day at approximately the same time. Regularity helps students worry less about something that could suddenly come up to disrupt their day, so that, instead, they can mentally prepare for times when they need to concentrate on learning.*
>
> *Several times each day in her classroom, Ms. Montoya gives students a few minutes of quiet reflection time. During these calming reflection periods, Ms. Montoya lets students draw, write, or just think about how their day is going and how they have been able to manage their emotions. Even students who aren't currently in traumatic situations benefit from these opportunities to reflect on their day. This helps all students develop the skill of compartmentalization to help them build resilience. By putting stressors "away" and reflecting on how they have managed them, students have a better chance of managing them in the future. This self-correction process helps students handle stressful situations and increase their resilience.*

Throughout this chapter, you have examined the practices Ms. Montoya implements to help establish a classroom culture that is accepting and nurturing not only for trauma-impacted students but also for *all* her students. None of these practices have caused Ms. Montoya to compromise her core beliefs or standards, but they have improved her professional practice. She has found that what is good for students experiencing trauma is also good for *all* the students she serves.

Conclusion

In this chapter, we discussed several ideas to help you understand and manage the emotions associated with trauma-impacted students. First, we looked briefly at several areas of the brain and their primary functions. We also examined the impact of trauma on the brain and the reactions people have when they are in dangerous or traumatic situations. As a teacher, it's important for you to have this knowledge so you can spot signs of various reactions when they appear.

We also looked at some straightforward and foundational strategies teachers can use for all students (not just trauma-impacted students) to help provide the classroom culture needed for students to experience learning success. It's important that these aspects match the culture of the classroom, the needs of the students, and the teaching style of the teacher.

Understanding how the brain works and its reactions to trauma is helpful in our work with all students. The ideas and strategies you have learned are just the beginning or tip of the iceberg. As you grow in your own professional practice working with trauma-impacted students, you'll refine and develop many more strategies.

In chapter 4 (page 67), you'll discover ways to make positive connections with the trauma-impacted students you serve. While these strategies are designed to engage students coming from traumatic situations, they are also good practice to use with all students.

QUESTIONS FOR ***Reflection***

As you think about what you learned in this chapter and how it can be implemented in your classroom, reflect on the following questions.

- How does understanding the major brain regions help you understand how trauma impacts student thinking and learning? What big ideas did you learn that match your own experiences in the area of trauma-informed instruction?

- Why is the classroom culture so important in helping all students successfully learn and grow, particularly those who experience trauma?
- What are some simple ways you can begin to develop a positive and supportive classroom culture? How can you continue to develop this kind of classroom culture as you get to know your students at a more in-depth level?
- How do you plan to implement what you've learned in this chapter and share the ideas with your colleagues and administrators?

chapter four

Positive Relationships With Students

Mr. Juarez, a high school science teacher, knows that several of his students come from traumatic home situations. Some of their situations may help to explain (not excuse) their classroom behaviors. He understands that it may be hard for some of these students to develop a trusting relationship with him since the adults in their lives constantly break their trust. Mr. Juarez understands the importance of building genuine relationships with his students.

Mr. Juarez makes a point to welcome each of his students to his classroom. He also tries to understand their interests and incorporate them into his conversations and lessons. He makes positive comments about any upcoming activities his students may be involved in and he never engages in sarcasm. If there is ever a joke or funny comment, he makes sure it's focused on something related to him, one of his personal challenges, or something related to the science content. Because he works so hard to build relationships with students, Mr. Juarez is regularly chosen as one of the favorite teachers in student body surveys.

Mr. Juarez works hard to build relationships with his students, just like many of you do. Throughout this chapter, you'll discover that Mr. Juarez builds relationships with students for several specific reasons. One of these is to be able to help students as they face traumatic situations. In order for students to feel comfortable sharing with him, they need to have a sense of trust that goes beyond superficial teacher-student relationships. In this chapter, we'll examine strategies and ideas to develop a foundation of trust with students, as well as how to move to a deeper level of trust that those students experiencing trauma can use to reach out for support.

In this chapter, we explore relationship building and trust between teachers and students. These skills help teachers build better relationships with students than they may have had in the past. This higher level of trust will be useful as teachers work to support students experiencing childhood trauma.

Keep in mind that your relationship with students should be appropriate. By *appropriate*, we mean that as the adult, it's important for you to set and follow boundaries. For example, your relationship with a student might be focused on mentoring. This doesn't mean that you are there to be his or her friend. Students experiencing an abusive situation might not be comfortable getting too close (emotionally or physically). Make sure your relationships are appropriate and comfortable for both you and the students.

As you review the information in this chapter, be sure to focus on the following.

- The nature of trust and using it as a foundation to building relationships with students
- How focusing on students' strengths and assets help you build trust
- The power of sensitivity, tone, and caring in fostering relationships with students
- How to respond with the appropriate feedback when students regress or fall backward, separating the behavior from the people in a way that builds relationships

Positive relationships are crucial when working with students impacted by trauma. As a teacher, you get pressure to focus on academic skills, student achievement progress, and content. While academic skills and achievement are important, developing students' personalities, decision-making skills, and ability to work well with others are also crucial for success both inside and outside the classroom.

The Importance of Building Positive Relationships With Students

In our own personal and professional lives, we both see the value of relationships. Growing up in homes where we experienced multiple and ongoing traumas, we had to develop resilience. In order to survive and thrive, we knew we had to find ways to cope with these traumatic situations and compartmentalize them so they would not impact our focus in school, in sports, and in our careers. Recognizing what a positive relationship is and learning to form and maintain these kinds of relationships became part of our resilience. Additionally, beyond developing resilience to cope with the situations we were facing, we also had to develop the skills to know how to be what Steven R. Covey (2013) calls *transition people.* People tend to duplicate the same environments they experience as children when they become adults. There are multigenerational examples of alcohol abuse, child neglect, and other very negative situations.

Since children in trauma tend to see their environment as somewhat normal, they might duplicate the same environment when they grow into adults and have their own families. This is what our parents did—they duplicated the environment they experienced as children. If we had done the same, our own families and children might have experienced alcoholism, verbal and physical abuse, and neglect as they grew. When educators build positive relationships with students, they help students see different models than they may be experiencing at home. A new model can show students that there's another way to be adults than the way the abusers in their lives are. When students see educators as role models, it can help them envision the transition out of trauma they could make when they become adults.

In our cases, influential teachers reached out to form positive relationships with us that helped us see what was possible and *transition* ourselves out of these negative and dangerous situations. As adults, we made sure to guide our families as well as we could to keep them safe and away from similar circumstances.

As a teacher, you can also serve as a transition person for some of your students. When you reach out, seek to develop appropriate relationships, and serve in a mentor role, you increase your chances to help students transition out of trauma in the future.

Because parents are the primary adults with whom children initially strive to build relationships, when this becomes difficult, they reach out to others to fill the gap. Many children can then develop unhealthy relationships, such as caustic friendships or affiliations with gangs. Some children are so desperate for relationships that they can't recognize a negative influence. By developing relationships with their teachers, students might receive the attention and care they need and diminish the need for some of these other harmful relationships.

Trust

At the foundation of all meaningful relationships is trust. People earn trust through consistency over time. In your own personal relationships, you may find those who you trust the most have almost developed a track record with you. They are interested in you. They are there when you need them. They consistently do what they say they will do, and they rarely disappoint you. In *Creative Strategies to Transform School Culture,* Eller and Eller (2009) discuss *trust* as the summation of many incidents of positive interactions between two people. The trust you build with your students is then the sum of your many consistent interactions with them.

Notably, building trust with trauma-impacted students can present its own unique challenges. In the article, "Helping Children Cope With Traumatic Events," HelpGuide (n.d.) states, "Trauma can alter the way a child or teen sees the world, making it suddenly seem a much more dangerous and frightening place. [Students] may find it more difficult to trust both their environment and other people." Therefore, trauma-impacted students may need help to rebuild a sense of safety and security beyond what a typical student might require.

Covey (2013), author of *The Seven Habits of Highly Effective People*, shares the concept of building a trusting relationship based on a series of positive interactions; he calls the concept an *emotional bank account.*

"Deposits" in Emotional Bank Accounts

According to Covey (2013), with each relationship, people start on a neutral basis. As one continues to interact with the other person, he or she experiences positive as well as not-so-positive emotional experiences. With each positive experience, one builds a positive perception of that other person and trust grows. When something negative happens, that negative experience diminishes one's sense of trust.

Over time, the total of the positive experiences and the negative experiences acts like a bank account. If the total of the positive experiences is greater, you may feel you have a better relationship with that person. Because you have more positive interactions, and you trust the other person, you may be better able to disregard an occasional negative experience.

Let's see how this principle works in Mr. Juarez's classroom.

In his classroom, Mr. Juarez works hard to build relationships by purposely having more initial positive interactions with his students. At the start of the school year, his science outcomes are less complex than those he teaches later in the school year, so he finds ways to recognize students for their academic efforts as much as possible. Also, student behavior can be better at the start of the year, so he tries to also recognize students for their behavior efforts. In both academic and behavior issues, Mr. Juarez builds relationships by building emotional bank accounts with students.

After a few weeks, Claudia, one of Mr. Juarez's students, gets off task during a lesson. Mr. Juarez talks with her about the incident after class and tells her why her behavior was not appropriate for the situation. He addresses her behavior, not her personality, in his feedback. Because Mr. Juarez has spent time developing a relationship with her and made the emotional bank account positive in the past, Claudia listens to what he has to say and then shares what happened at home in the morning that upset her.

Claudia's mom came home from a date and had been drinking. She was on the phone with her boyfriend arguing until 3:00 a.m. While getting ready for school, Claudia's mom yelled at Claudia and told her she had to get her two little sisters ready for school. This incident upset Claudia and impacted her classroom behavior. Mr. Juarez thanks Claudia for sharing, and they work together to develop a way for her to let him know when there is an issue like this in the future so he can help Claudia keep her behavior on track.

In this example, you get a glimpse of the concepts of trust and emotional bank accounts in action. Because Mr. Juarez spends so much time developing relationships with his students and making positive deposits in their emotional bank accounts, the students understand that he has their best interests in mind. They know he *has their backs* and will help them with challenging situations. Claudia feels comfortable telling him about a very personal (and embarrassing) incident and then works with him to develop a strategy to help her in the future.

Without this level of trust, some students follow your direction only because of your position of authority. If Mr. Juarez had not made many positive deposits in Claudia's emotional bank account, she may have not shared what had happened to her or may have even become defiant when he approached her. If Claudia decided to clam up or escalate the situation by becoming aggressive or obstinate, the situation could have quickly gotten out of control.

Building trust with students does not guarantee you'll always be able to find out what has happened to impact the incident or that certain situations won't get out of control, but trust will help you build stronger relationships with students so they feel they can depend on you.

"Withdrawals" From Emotional Bank Accounts

Covey (2013) states that when negative events occur (either purposeful or accidental), people make withdrawals from their emotional bank account. These negative experiences are based on the receiver's perception, not the intent. Scolding students, not listening intently, going back on your word, not following through on what you've promised, or a variety of other negative interactions could cause students to make a withdrawal from their emotional bank account. Sometimes, the student's reaction provides an indication that an emotional bank account withdrawal is happening. In other cases, students have become so good at self-protection that teachers have no indication students have made this withdrawal.

Trauma-impacted students most likely experience emotional bank account withdrawals frequently. Adults in their lives may disappoint them a lot. An adult might verbally abuse them and then apologize, promising never to do it again, only to strike out the next time he or she is upset. Or maybe a parent fails to pick up a student from school because he or she overslept after a drug or alcohol binge, leaving the student standing outside all alone. When the parent finally shows up, he or she yells at the child for standing where others can see. While these and other emotional withdrawals happen, children may appear to recover and move on, but the negative experiences add up. Covey (2013) contends it may take several positive deposits to compensate for one negative withdrawal.

Your relationships have a foundation in this concept of emotional bank accounts. As you work with students to develop and nurture relationships, you must monitor your deposits and withdrawals. All the positive comments you give students, the times you listen intently, the smiles you give them when they complete a task, and the times when you do what you say you are going to do, are positive deposits and help develop your relationships with students. At times, when you have to give students developmental feedback, redirect them, or cause some other emotional bank account withdrawal, there's a potential of diminishing the relationships. It's important to observe students' reactions when you are delivering constructive feedback to see if they are reacting negatively.

In the initial stages of developing relationships with students, you need to be careful to maximize early emotional bank account deposits and minimize withdrawals. Research shows it can take at least five positive statements to compensate for one negative statement (Zenger & Folkman, 2013). Whatever the ratio, teachers need to think about making multiple deposits for each withdrawal.

Once you have developed strong relationships, you can help students realize that not all feedback and redirection is necessarily negative. In strong relationships, people may offer advice or tell others what they need to improve to help them to grow. In these kinds of situations, the feedback should be clear, specific, and based on the behavior, not the person. Later, we'll look at ideas to provide good, constructive, developmental feedback that grows a relationship rather than diminishes it.

A Focus on Student Assets

Everyone likes people who focus on others' strengths and minimize the negative aspects. Similarly, having a bright outlook and focusing on students' strengths can have a significant and positive impact on students' self-esteem.

As a teenager, one of Tom's favorite comedic acts was the Monty Python troupe. In the movie *Monty Python's Life of Brian* (Goldstone & Jones, 1979), Eric Idle sings a song called "Always Look on the Bright Side of Life," which states: "When you're chewing on life's gristle, don't grumble, give a whistle!" (Goldstone & Jones, 1979). The song goes on, giving examples of how to always look on the bright side of life.

Tom often sang these lyrics in his head as he faced challenging situations in the classroom, using this practice to calm himself. It's not always easy to see the bright side in the heat of the moment, but if you accept the idea that behavior is a form of communication, then you must accept that sometimes communication is negative, and you can't overcome it with more negative. It's frustrating, however, and educators also know this to be true: being positive does not guarantee a good result but being negative seems to ensure a bad one. When a teacher responds negatively to an already negative student, this can cause further spiraling and an absolute departure from any potential resolution. Some trauma-impacted students have learned to protect themselves by either not reacting (hide behavior) or by verbally or physically striking out (fight behavior).

Focusing on students' assets means that educators build on the strengths students have as they support students' continued growth. In *Seven Keys to a Positive Learning Environment in Your Classroom*, Hierck (2017) suggests educators remember that "every student comes into the classroom with his or her own **s**trengths, **t**alents, **o**pportunities for growth, **r**esources, and **y**earnings (STORY). When teachers know each student's STORY, they can offer feedback tailored to that student" (p. 48).

Positive, proactive discipline takes time; negative, reactive discipline takes even more time because teachers must invest time repairing the damage done by this kind of discipline. When students are struggling, they need adults to model desired behaviors. There is always a positive way to respond to a situation, and responding in this way is an important part of modeling positive behaviors for students. A positive attitude is the key to creating positive, supportive classrooms and schools that produce happy and successful students. What can you identify as the "bright side" of each student in your classroom? Take time to identify strengths and assets in each student, and remind yourself of those strengths when students are having bad moments.

Let's see how this principle works in Mr. Juarez's classroom.

> *Mr. Juarez knows that one of his students, Devin, comes from a single-parent home where the dad is working two jobs to make a living. He knows Devin is in charge of the younger siblings most weeknight evenings and is not able to participate in many of the outside activities other students are able to do. While Devin is quiet and shy, Mr. Juarez also knows he is well organized.*
>
> *As Mr. Juarez has gotten to know Devin, he has learned that he strives for attention from adults. Mr. Juarez decides to ask Devin to help him set up labs in his classroom before school and during his free period each day. As Devin works to make sure the lab equipment is set up properly, Mr. Juarez praises him by letting him know specifically why his work is so good. Devin develops a trusting relationship with Mr. Juarez, and Mr. Juarez reinforces that relationship by acknowledging other things Devin does well. As time goes on, Mr. Juarez brings in a few other students to help, and Devin develops relationships with them and starts to talk with them outside of the lab setup situation.*
>
> *By looking at the good, rather than focusing on the problems Devin has outside of school, Mr. Juarez helps Devin be more confident and relaxed around the other students. The relationships Devin*

forms with other students in the lab can continue through social media during his out-of-school time, while he's taking care of his siblings, for instance. Devin learns that he has classmates who have similar responsibilities for siblings as he does, and because of this, he feels less alone.

This scenario demonstrates how recognizing the strengths or assets of a student, and then developing those strengths, can both build the relationship and help the student grow. As Mr. Juarez works with Devin, he focuses on strengths and uses this relationship to help Devin branch out to other students.

John was once doing some work and a seminar in an area where neighborhood shootings occurred on a weekly basis. When the cab driver dropped him off at the school for the first time, he told John that they normally don't come to this area at night because of the danger. During the seminar, some of the teachers shared concerns they had with student behaviors in their classrooms, in the halls, and around the school. John asked the teachers to brainstorm and identify some of the situations the students were facing at home and outside of school, then list all the positive attributes and strengths of their students. When the teachers stepped back and looked at the list of challenges compared to the students' positive attributes or behaviors, they were shocked. In spite of rampant violence, drug abuse, conflict, and fear in the neighborhood, most of the students were friendly, vocal, and had developed talents such as singing, dancing, and drawing.

The teachers and the principal decided to start looking at the gifts the students brought to school rather than the troubles they might cause. The school leadership team helped identify key classroom and school changes that focused on students' strengths rather than trying to make students fit the school's expectations. For example, classroom settings incorporated more movement and interactions rather than lectures and presentations, and teachers decided to recognize student assets to help build relationships.

Over time, teachers noticed a better school and classroom environment. Because they focused on the positive, they were making deposits in the students' emotional bank accounts (see page 70). Providing a high ratio of positive deposits enabled them to develop better working relationships with students. The students started to realize that the teachers were interested in them and their success. The situation wasn't perfect. Teachers and administrators still had to deal with discipline, attendance, aggression, and other issues. However, these issues occurred less frequently, and staff dealt with them differently than in the past.

Focusing on the positive attributes of students enabled the staff at this school to begin to build lasting and long-term relationships with students that made a difference in their lives. Since many of these relationships were lacking in the students' home environments, the students greatly benefited from these positive relationships with their teachers.

Sensitivity

The following quote, attributed to Theodore Roosevelt, offers a great reminder about the foundation of every successful classroom: "Nobody cares how much you know, until they know how much you care" (BrainyQuote, n.d.). Showing sensitivity toward each student's unique needs, backgrounds, and experiences goes a long way in showing that you care about them.

According to Michael Roberts (2019), quality educators invest time and effort to get to know their students, showing they care about them both inside and outside of the classroom. Relationships are the foundation of good teaching in any classroom. All students have unique skills, experiences, talents, and gifts that can enrich the classroom. Invent time to understand what students value as well as their strengths and individual needs. Engage in conversations, give student surveys to gain information, or ask questions on exit slips. Learn about students' hobbies and interests so you can use that information when planning your lessons. It's important to do as much as you can to understand each student as a unique and complex individual, beyond his or her physical or cultural identity. This demonstrates that you are sensitive to students' individual needs.

As a teacher, you set the tone for your classroom. Your actions define what is embraced and encouraged, and what is unacceptable and needs to change. The focus is on developing in students the skills to change behavior not their individuality. This is a big job, and one that requires you to be aware of any biases you carry into the classroom.

Tone is especially important to students living in traumatic conditions in their homes or neighborhoods. In a trauma-filled home, there may not be a feeling of safety. The environment may be unstable or dangerous. So, remember to be sensitive to the tone you convey, ensuring students feel safe and respected in your classroom.

Caring and Understanding

As an extension of communicating sensitivity, it's important that students know that the adults both care for and understand the unique experiences each child brings to the class. Get to know your students and the lives they live both inside and outside school, especially if your students are from different cultural or socioeconomic backgrounds than you may be used to. In the busy world of schools, it may not always be possible to meet every student individually, so take some initial steps such as asking students to complete an interest inventory. This can be as simple as asking students to write down their five favorite activities, movies, music groups, hobbies, sports, and so on. Their responses can help you make the curriculum more relevant to their lives—a sure method for letting students know you care about them.

Getting to know students and their lives outside of school will help you understand students as a "whole picture." By seeking to learn more about what your students may be experiencing, you gain important knowledge that helps you *understand* them not *excuse* their behaviors. As you learn more about what students may be experiencing outside of school, you gain perspective about how well they are functioning *in spite of* their home situations.

Another great strategy to show students you care is to ensure you are an active listener. The skill of active listening is closely related to the skill introduced earlier—temporary suspension of opinion. Teachers who actively listen to students are listening for the meaning *behind* what students are saying and then check to make sure they've understood correctly. This level of listening may not be happening in students' home lives. Listening carefully and with intent supports students' dignity and confidence, and helps develop trusting relationships between teachers and students (Thomas et al., 2019).

If you are truly listening, you are doing so openly and intentionally in order to understand students. Sometimes it's effective to share something about yourself with students to show them you can relate to them or that you understand their situation. However, be careful to ensure you don't immediately reflect on your own personal experiences. This could lead to making assumptions about students' backgrounds based on your own childhood, resulting in students receiving care more aligned with your experience as an adult than with them.

The Significant 72 website (www.significant72.com) has numerous activities educators can use to build relationships with their students and demonstrate caring and understanding.

Humor Without Sarcasm

Another way to build caring relationships with students is to use humor in your conversations and in your teaching. Everyone likes to have fun and see the lighter side of life. A teacher might decide to start each class with a joke of the day. While these jokes can be corny and somewhat old, students will laugh and poke fun at the teacher for telling them. As we noted earlier, it's OK to poke fun at yourself or the content; however, it's not OK to poke fun at the students.

This brings up the topic of sarcasm. Some teachers of secondary school (junior high, middle school, and high school) students think that because students are older, they can understand sarcasm and accept it from their teachers. Sarcasm can be very dangerous and almost always weakens relationships. Students may appear to laugh and go along with the sarcastic joke, but deep down, they may feel anger and a sense of betrayal when someone says something sarcastic about them.

Even as adults, we do not value sarcasm. John remembers a colleague who retired after a long tenure as a school district leader. At his retirement party, the current superintendent included sarcasm related to some of the work he was describing in his speech to honor the retiring administrator. While some members of the group thought the comments were funny, the retiring administrator did not. His feelings were hurt, and he was left with some lasting memories that were less than positive. The administrator appeared not to be bothered by the sarcastic remarks. Years later, when John met him at a coffee shop, the retired administrator let him know that he was still upset about the sarcastic remarks.

If a competent adult still has negative feelings years later about sarcastic remarks, think about how a thirteen-year-old student might react to such remarks. The best practice is to *never* use sarcasm with students. It's a potential relationship destroyer. Focus on positive attributes and ways to build students' feelings of self-worth. They will be grateful for your positive comments and support.

Feedback to Build Relationships

Earlier in this chapter, we talked about the role of feedback in developing and building relationships. While purely positive comments can help establish trust in a relationship, feedback is necessary for the relationship to grow. In *Flip This School*, the authors share ideas about providing feedback to adults (Eller & Eller, 2019). Teachers can use these same strategies to provide feedback to students as well. In the following sections, we share some of those ideas.

Reinforcing Feedback

When teachers give students reinforcing feedback, they are attempting to help them understand a positive or productive behavior and either continue to use it or strengthen its use. For example, if you see that a student is well organized for class, you'll want him or her to build on this skill to become even more organized.

In general, to recognize and strengthen a behavior, it's important to be clear and specific, identify the behavior, and recommend its continued use. In providing reinforcing feedback to build relationships, we recommend the following process.

1. Provide clear and specific feedback. Focus more on the behavior and less on the person.
2. Provide examples of the behavior and the impact the behavior has on others or the situation.
3. Encourage the student to continue the behavior.

Here's how this feedback may sound in a real situation: "Amy, thank you for coming to class today and starting on your work right away. I noticed that it increased your focus and helped you get ready for the rest of the day. I expect that you'll keep doing this in the future."

This example illustrates the value of specific feedback. While general feedback, such as "Good job" or "I like the way you came into class today," may sound more positive, but as the relationship grows, specific feedback is more helpful.

When developing and sharing reinforcing feedback, it's important that it is sincere and honest. Making something up or sharing feedback because it's on the student's schedule diminishes its power and the relationship. Be honest and sincere when working with your students.

Developmental Feedback

Another important aspect to building stronger relationships with students is the ability to share feedback designed to help students grow. In *Flip this School*, Eller and Eller (2019) discuss the concept of *developmental feedback*. Even though developmental feedback is presented in the context of providing growth feedback to teachers, the clear and specific feedback designed to promote growth also can be helpful to students.

Adapted from Eller and Eller (2019), you should keep the following points in mind when giving developmental feedback.

- Describe the specific behavior that the student needs to focus on or change.
- Share examples (from observation or experience) that illustrate the behavior the student must change.
- Provide the rationale for the change.
- State the new or desired behavior that should replace the problematic behavior. If you believe it will be helpful, share examples of what the new behavior will look like in the classroom.
- Check for understanding of the new expectations the student must implement. Use open-ended questions, and ask the student to be clear in his or her understanding. Re-explain if needed.
- Share your wishes and some opportunities to follow up to check on or support the change.

Trauma-impacted students can benefit from this type of feedback because it is clear, specific, and provides direction for making changes. They may not receive this type of feedback at home; if they do, it may be negative or condescending.

Here's how developmental feedback may sound in a real situation: "Tony, I noticed you haven't been getting started on the posted work right away when you come into the room. I need you to get started right away, so I can see if you understand the material or if I need to help you with your work. *(Pause for student response.)* Please tell me, what am I looking for you to do when you come into the classroom in the future? *(Pause for student response.)* Thanks, I'll check in with you next week to see how things are going."

The example is simple but illustrates the concepts important to developmental feedback. It might seem easier just to say, "Get to work!" but carefully explaining the needed change helps the student understand what he or she needs to do plus keeps you in the positive, helpful mode. When you explain things with more detail, it's often easier to stay calm. If you deliver the feedback in a calm and supportive manner, you model a stable tone of voice and reinforce predictability. This is a relationship-building strategy you can use once you have developed a foundational-level relationship with a student.

Conclusion

In this chapter, we discussed many ideas and strategies to build relationships with students. While building positive and productive relationships with all students is good, building these relationships with students experiencing trauma is especially important. You may be the only adult they can count on to have their best interests at heart.

Relationships are at the center of the work you do to impact your students. Devoting time to build relationships will pay off, leading to better situations for students, higher levels of learning and achievement, and more resilient and happy learners.

In chapter 5 (page 83), we'll examine practices and strategies to successfully manage your classroom so it is more *trauma friendly* or helps trauma-impacted students be more successful. As you review this chapter, reflect on how you can integrate the ideas on relationship building into your existing classroom management practices. As with all the trauma-sensitive practices we present in this book, they work well with all students to promote their success and sense of belonging in your classroom.

QUESTIONS FOR ***Reflection***

As you think about what you learned in this chapter and how it can be implemented in your classroom, reflect on the following questions.

- Why is building relationships so important for students experiencing trauma? How do relationships help these students move beyond trauma and make positive connections with adults?

- What are some ways you are already building relationships with your students? How could you enhance these strategies to reach *all* students, especially trauma-impacted students?
- Why is it important to look at the strengths and assets each student brings to your classroom? How can understanding the situations they face and using their assets help build relationships with trauma-impacted students?
- What have you learned about the importance of feedback, and how can you use feedback to shape your professional practice?

chapter five

Trauma-Sensitive Classroom Management Strategies and Techniques

An eighth-grade student named Myrna has been assigned to Monroe Middle School after her third different foster family placement. Monroe's Principal Jones meets with each eighth-grade team in Myrna's new school. During these meetings, Principal Jones describes Myrna's background and experiences in her other schools. She has gotten into trouble within a short time after she started at each school. Myrna always seemed to find a student to fight with, something to steal, or got into an argument with one of her teachers. Afterward, she was moved to another foster family and yet another school.

After the meetings, the Blue Team says it would like to work with Myrna. The Blue Team is composed of teachers who work with a specific group of students throughout the year. Together, these students and teachers are known as the Blue Team. Principal Jones and the Blue Team decide to invite Myrna to meet them the next afternoon. At this introduction meeting, Myrna and her foster parents come to school to meet members of the Blue Team. They introduce themselves, but they want to know more about Myrna. They ask her about how she best likes to learn, her favorite subjects, where she likes to sit in class, and other things they think would help her feel welcome. This is the first school and the first time teachers have shown an interest in Myrna. Myrna is nervous but feels a little more comfortable on her first day since she was able to meet the teachers and the teachers showed interest in her needs.

The actions of the teachers in this part of Myrna's story illustrate an awareness of trauma and of the importance of relationships. Principal Jones provided his teachers with support and professional development in how to understand trauma and help set up an environment for all students to be successful, especially those experiencing trauma. First, Principal Jones involved school teams in the decision of where to place Myrna. Since the Blue Team selected her, it will be more invested in her success. The Blue Team members decide to meet with Myrna first, by themselves, to begin to get to know her and help her feel more relaxed about coming to school. Since Myrna has been to so many schools and foster families, she had developed a sense that she is not welcome. By making her entrance into the school seem special, team members reinforce that they are interested in working with her.

This initial meeting is just the beginning of what team members will do to help Myrna feel like part of the group and valued by her teachers. By taking the first positive step, they are being proactive in building a relationship with Myrna. As described later in this chapter, helping Myrna be successful will take a lot of work and love on the part of her teachers.

In this chapter, you'll learn to plan and implement classroom management strategies to help *all* students, including those who are trauma impacted, be successful and thrive in your classroom.

As you review the information in this chapter, be sure to focus on the following.

- How to build a sense of community in your classroom
- The impact of stress on a student's brain and taking that into consideration when working with students who are disruptive or off task
- Strategies and techniques to avoid confrontations, focusing on the behavior rather than the student's personality when working with off-task behaviors
- How to avoid power struggles and manage potentially dangerous situations with trauma-impacted students

Classroom management serves not only to keep order in the classroom but also to help students increase their learning and self-management skills. If you approach classroom management with trauma-impacted students in mind, you'll make your classroom a more productive place for them and all the other students you work with on a daily basis. Effective classroom management will prevent or head off potential issues and make your room a great place for students to learn and for you to work.

Focus on Student Learning Needs

At the foundation of every well-managed classroom is the focus on student learning needs. Imagine student behavior as an energy source, such as a water current, the following analogy will help illustrate this concept.

Let's say that student behavior is like a stream. It flows in a certain manner or direction based on the need of the water to flow toward a larger river. You can try to stop or change the water flow for a short time, but with the first major rainstorm, the water goes back to its preferred path. No matter what kinds of changes or controls you place on the stream, it will eventually resume its natural or preferred path.

In a classroom of students, there is a natural energy flow as well. This energy is based on many things but has a foundation in student learning needs. For example, in an early childhood classroom, students need to integrate movement into their learning. We have found it's important to incorporate some type of movement into learning activities at all grade levels. If educators teach by having students sit and listen passively for extended periods of time, they aren't really attuned to students' individual needs.

When working with trauma-impacted students, teachers need to take their specific needs (physical, social, and emotional) into consideration. As noted previously, trauma-impacted students may have unmet needs in their home environment they are looking to meet in your classroom. For example, in Myrna's scenario at the beginning of this chapter, you learn that Myrna had attended many schools and had lived in several foster homes. She might have a great need for attachment to others, especially adults. The Blue Team took this need into consideration when members decided to meet her outside the school day without the other students present. They tried to provide Myrna with a chance to connect with them.

Identify Teaching Needs

Just focusing on student needs when building a successful trauma-sensitive classroom environment will not be effective if you don't take into account your teaching needs as well. You'll want to find a way to blend students' needs and your teaching needs together for the perfect balance.

For example, if you teach primarily by presenting small bits of information, then involve students in discussing this information in small groups, think about how you can help students learn how to hold meaningful discussions. If you operate your classroom by asking students to use manipulatives and hands-on activities, then make sure students know and exhibit behavior skills such as voice-level control, and the ability to work in small groups as needed for these learning methods to be successful in your classroom.

In Myrna's scenario, the Blue Team members used a lot of interactive strategies, such as small-group and partner activities, to increase interaction in their classrooms. Since all team members shared similar teaching methods, they worked together to develop similar or common expectations. Since their students would be doing a lot of partner or small-group discussions, they worked hard to develop learning communities in their classrooms. Because the Blue Team operates as a learning community, the teachers felt assured that the students would accept Myrna.

These teachers worked to integrate the learning needs of their students with their own teaching needs. For example, teachers needed to establish an organized classroom structure to ensure a stable learning environment, and students needed a safe and predictable learning environment, so teachers developed structures to provide organization and stability. Teachers needed a way to gauge students' emotional state at the start of the day, and students needed a method to communicate their emotions, so teachers developed a check-in process in which students could place their names on a bulletin board in areas that described their emotions. In both of these examples, the teachers tailored their strategies to meet both their teaching needs and students' learning needs.

Establish and Clearly Communicate Expectations

Trauma-impacted students can live in home environments that are totally out of their control. They can't do anything about a family member who drops them off at events and then forgets to pick them up for hours, or a parent who's working two to three jobs in order to make a living and isn't able to help his or her children with homework or make sure they have clean clothes to wear to school.

You may find that these trauma-impacted students need to have some control over their learning environment. Involving them in helping set some of the parameters related to classroom expectations can help them gain some level of control. In our own classrooms and those of teachers we have worked with, allowing students to participate in setting classroom expectations was successful because not only did they enjoy being involved in the process but they also felt a sense of ownership. Students exhibited more positive behaviors and became more responsible for addressing issues when they arose.

While involving students in setting expectations can be helpful, in some situations, you may find it advantageous to provide more direction. For example, if you don't think students have the skills or discipline to assist in establishing classroom parameters, you may want to establish some first, as samples. As the school year progresses, if you notice students gaining specific skills of ownership and responsibility, you could involve them on a deeper level.

Teachers who work with students to develop shared expectations tell us they get more commitment from their students in the learning environment. This increased commitment could be due to the ownership students gain when they help construct the classroom environment. The shared expectation development process is especially helpful for trauma-impacted children since their level of control in situations outside of school may be diminished. In addition, all students benefit from an engagement in the shared expectations as it helps them work toward becoming independent, self-directed learners. Developing classroom expectations is not a one-size-fits-all approach. The process should be based on students' unique learning needs, strengths, and limitations, and what fits the natural rhythm of your classroom. The unique nature of students' management needs can make setting expectations and behavior parameters challenging but effective when done collaboratively.

In *Seven Keys to a Positive Learning Environment in Your Classroom*, Hierck (2017) shares the importance of communicating expectations for the learning environment: "Every year, each classroom must establish expectations, routines, predictable structures, and first steps toward creating a learning community where *all* students become proficient in the desired outcomes (behavior and academics)" (p. 19).

Setting clear expectations is one of the most important activities a teacher engages in during the first few days of school. If teachers can clearly explain expectations, it helps students understand how the classroom will operate to maximize their learning opportunities. Teachers should not only explain expectations but also check to make sure students understand them. Students might repeat the expectations, discuss them in small groups, post them on chart paper, or even create a skit or "newscast" to demonstrate their understanding.

Create a Classroom Learning Community

In this section, we explore the concept of building a classroom learning community. This is a crucial concept for success related to classroom management. Many teachers of trauma-impacted students have found this concept helpful to their work.

In a community, many different people with different strengths and challenges work together for the benefit of everyone. There are people who take care of maintenance, others who help get water and electricity to community members, some help provide education, and still others help to get food and other supplies to their fellow community members. In the end, everyone works together for the benefit of everyone in the community.

A classroom learning community is similar to a community where people live together. Students use their unique strengths and talents to help everyone be successful. Classroom learning communities have common expectations, find ways to regularly check how they are doing in relation to these expectations, and recalibrate their behaviors to get back to their base expectations. Classroom learning communities come together to make changes and adjustments when the learning environment changes.

For example, the Blue Team at Monroe Middle School holds periodic classroom meetings to recalibrate its community expectations. Let's see how this works when Myrna joins the learning community at Monroe.

> *Tuesday is Myrna's first day in her new school. The Blue Team decides it is a good idea to hold a morning meeting to welcome her to school and help her understand classroom expectations. During the first hour, homeroom is scheduled. In homeroom, twenty-five students from the Blue Team welcome Myrna. While this welcome session is a little uncomfortable at first, Myrna gradually starts to*

feel welcome. It is helpful for her to hear from three other relatively new students as they share their experiences becoming part of the school's community.

Because the initial introduction session goes well, the Blue Team teachers decide it is OK for Myrna to meet all the Blue Team students. They all gather in the common area to meet her. During this session, the students welcome Myrna and review the expectations and procedures they have been using in their learning community. Several students offer to help her by showing her around and answering questions during her first few days of school. Myrna feels welcome in her new school.

In this example, the teachers and students help set a welcoming tone for Myrna during her initial time in their school. This takes place right away to help her get off to a good start. Myrna has never experienced this type of welcome before, so it takes her by surprise.

Myrna had developed issues related to trust and belonging in the past so it will take her time to change her normal reaction to school. She may regress in her behavior and may even misbehave or strike out when something bad happens. By reaching out to Myrna and welcoming her, the Blue Team makes a huge emotional bank account deposit. Many more deposits will be needed in order for Myrna to feel safer and more connected. Even though each member of the Blue Team learning community is different, all work together to provide a safe and welcoming atmosphere.

Use Consistent Processes and Procedures

In *Thriving as a New Teacher*, the authors talk about the importance of helping students learn and practice behaviors (Eller & Eller, 2016). You can't assume students come to your classroom possessing the skills to behave the way you'd like them to, just like you can't assume students come to school with the academic skills you are trying to teach them in your class.

Students impacted by trauma may have learned a set of skills to survive their traumatic experiences (similar to the fight, flight, hide, freeze, or appease behaviors discussed earlier) and may have difficulty in following or using typical classroom procedures. For example, a student who has had to deal with a parent who has a drug or alcohol addiction may not have seen appropriate decision-making modeled. He or she may think that making a short-term decision and taking the easiest approach to deal with a problem is what people do when facing difficult decisions. It's up to educators to help these students learn how to make appropriate decisions. They can learn through educators' modeling of appropriate behaviors, teaching them the steps for positive behaviors, practicing, and using behavior skills in classroom situations.

In *Thriving as a New Teacher*, Eller and Eller (2016) introduce a list of core behavior skills important to general classroom success, as shown in figure 5.1. To help students learn and practice these behaviors, treat them almost the same as academic learning by developing lessons or learning opportunities. For example, as mentioned earlier, you can begin by providing a stable and predictable classroom environment. Students should be able to count on the fact that they can predict their classroom will always be a safe place for them. As a part of stability or predictability, teachers should have a calm and consistent way to get everyone's attention in class. Developing a common signal for attention or desired behaviors is one way to help students stay on task and predict their environment.

Some examples of common signals include:

- Use the phrase, "I need your attention, please," and wait for students to be quiet.
- Clap your hands in a rhythmic pattern, and ask students to repeat the pattern.
- Ring a bell or chime.
- Turn down the lights in the room.
- Play a two- to three-second song segment and then stop.
- Move to the front of the room, hold up your hand, and pause.

These are just a few of the ideas we have seen teachers use to effectively signal the need for attention. By using a signal, you are providing a consistent and stable way to help students focus their attention. While this practice is good for trauma-impacted students, it is beneficial for all students. Being able to respond to a signal for attention is not something most students innately know, so teachers should teach, reinforce, and practice this skill with students until it becomes commonplace or a habit.

Use the following checklist to determine the self-management skills you want to focus on in your classroom.

- Skills to help students establish, maintain, or regain focus in the classroom:
  - o Students are able to stop what they are doing and respond to a signal for attention.
  - o Students are able to use appropriate voice levels in class and while involved in learning activities.
- Students know how to follow the prescribed procedures for routine tasks with minimal teacher direction:
  - o Students can work on assigned tasks continuously without allowing themselves to be unnecessarily distracted.
  - o Students can begin assignments within a reasonable amount of time after the assignments are given.
  - o Students can return to task quickly after an interruption.
- Skills to help students effectively move around the learning environment when movement is required:
  - o Students can enter and leave the learning environment quickly and quietly without disrupting others.
  - o When given choices, students can select an appropriate place to complete work.
  - o Students can take care of personal needs such as restroom breaks, obtaining supplies and materials, and so on, without disrupting others and according to classroom procedures.
  - o When students need to move around the room, they can do so without interrupting others or their work progress.
- Skills needed to maximize student learning efforts:
  - o Students are able to choose appropriate activities that maximize their personal learning goals when given a choice.
  - o Students are able to select appropriate material and amount of material from a supply center in order to complete a task.
  - o After completing the task, students are able to return unneeded materials to the supply center.
  - o Students are able to select appropriate working groups that maximize their learning when given workgroup choices.
  - o Students are able to read and implement directions provided in work centers with minimal teacher direction.
  - o Students are able to keep personal and public work spaces organized and clean in order to find necessary materials.

Source: Eller & Eller, 2016, p. 85.

Figure 5.1: Checklist for student self-management skills.

Visit ***go.SolutionTree.com/behavior*** *for a free reproducible version of this figure.*

If teachers have no signal for attention or students don't know it or how to respond to it, the only way teachers can get attention is to raise their voice over the volume of the students. As children who grew up in trauma and in our own work with trauma-impacted students, we have noticed that raised voices can have a minimal impact. Trauma-impacted students may hear yelling and conflict at home and have learned how to tune it out. Or a raised voice might mean trouble and possible abuse is coming. Learning and using calm processes for transitions is crucial for success.

As you review the core behavior skills outlined in figure 5.1 (page 91), identify how each skill helps provide a foundation of predictability and safety for students.

Redirect Off-Task Behaviors

Because of the unpredictable and sometimes violent reactions trauma-impacted students encounter outside of school, try to use methods for behavior management that do not come across as aggressive. One such nonaggressive method involves redirecting off-task behaviors.

Let's see how Ms. Ginsberg, a member of the Monroe Middle School Blue Team, redirects Myrna to draw the least attention to her and preserve the relationship they have built over the last couple of weeks.

> *In her eighth-grade science class, Ms. Ginsberg uses a combination of labs and informational presentations to teach science concepts. In the classroom, there are always lab supplies within reach. While Ms. Ginsberg is presenting a unit on cells, she notices Myrna playing with a rubber hose and a glass tube from one of the lab stations. Ms. Ginsberg continues with her presentation, but when there's a short break in the content, she makes eye contact and signals* no *to Myrna. Ms. Ginsberg knows Myrna sees her, but she continues to play with the lab equipment. During the next short content break, Ms. Ginsberg walks slowly approaches Myrna, makes eye contact, and again signals* no. *This time, Myrna puts back the items and focuses her attention on the lesson.*

In this brief example, Ms. Ginsberg uses subtle redirection rather than calling out Myrna on her behavior in front of the entire class. By being subtle, Ms. Ginsberg helps Myrna save face while communicating that what she is doing is not OK. If

Myrna continues to play with the equipment, Ms. Ginsberg might need to increase the intensity of the redirection to obtain the desired behavior from Myrna.

This example shows that the key to redirection that does not feel aggressive or humiliating to the student is to start with and use the least intrusive or hostile intervention to change the behavior. In our experience, having a minimally intrusive way to redirect behavior is critical in working with trauma-impacted students since most of them live in a very reactionary or hostile environment. By using calming redirection techniques, teachers help maintain the stability of the classroom and keep it a safe place for all learners.

Initially, teachers can manage off-task behaviors by addressing them with low-level interventions. When working with all students, but especially those experiencing trauma, it's best to maintain a sense of balance and not escalate the situation. We have seen that the escalation of emotions can cause trauma-impacted students to move into the fight, flight, or hide mode. If the student is only able to react and not rationalize the situation, the situation can escalate out of control.

Figure 5.2 (page 94) offers some sample low-level calming redirection strategies. These strategies can help in addressing behaviors in a way that doesn't attract a lot of attention to individual students or increase the student's energy or stress related to the behaviors. This helps to keep the situation and the student calm.

As you can see from this sample list, these strategies are simple and don't attract a lot of attention but are powerful if used properly. They are based on the need to keep the classroom operating on an even keel without escalating emotions. Maintaining stable, calm classroom environments is essential for trauma-impacted students but can be beneficial for all students. Students learn more from what you do than what you tell them. By modeling calm, thoughtful management, you let them know you don't need anger or displays of power to control others. These types of management techniques also help students learn self-management skills. In our experience, when student see teachers calmly address potentially emotional situations, they can learn and implement the same ideas when dealing with challenges in their own lives.

- **Ignore behavior:** Sometimes, when you just ignore a behavior, it will diminish. In absence of attention, some behaviors just go away.
- **The look:** Pausing for a moment to give students a disapproving look can let them know their behavior is out of bounds. Following up later with a conversation helps reinforce the fact that they should avoid this behavior in the future.
- **Stop and pause:** Sometimes, stopping for a moment can redirect behaviors. The momentary silence can cause a slight discomfort, resulting in a decrease or end to the off-task behavior.
- **Freeze a gesture:** This is similar to the stop-and-pause strategy. Stopping in mid-sentence while holding your hand still in a stop gesture (palm of hand out toward to the class) or pointing away from your body (as if your gesture is frozen) can reinforce the need to get back on track.
- **Change voice speed or volume:** This can be effective with more than one student. Changing your voice causes a change in attention. This can bring one or more students back on task.
- **Use student's name in the lesson:** If a student is off-task, using his or her name in the lesson (not calling the student out) helps redirect behavior.
- **Private signal:** Teachers find that developing a private signal with students who are regularly off task provides a subtle and private reminder for them to get back on task. It's also a good idea to follow up later privately to discuss the situation with them.
- **Proximity:** Walking over and standing by the off-task student can help redirect his or her behavior. For some students, your presence is something they'd like to avoid. Others may like the attention they get when you stand by them.
- **Write something down:** Sometimes, just pausing and writing something down when you notice off-task behavior can help redirect students. You could do this on a piece of paper on your desk, at a podium, or somewhere else convenient for you, so it doesn't take too much time away from the lesson. You don't need to make a big deal out of it; but make sure the student sees you writing. As with some of the other redirection strategies, you may want to follow up privately later with the student.

Figure 5.2: Sample low-level, calming redirection strategies.

Visit ***go.SolutionTree.com/behavior*** *for a free reproducible version of this figure.*

Provide Choices

A key to helping students get back on track in emotional situations is to focus on the behavior, not the person. In our work, we find that providing opportunities for choice can be an effective way to move focus from the person to behavior. Statements such as the following demonstrate how to provide choices to students.

- "You can stay here and reflect or move to the quiet area to reflect."
- "You can work with me on this now, or we can talk after class."
- "You can start on your work right away or start with me after school."

All these statements are an attempt to take out emotion, depersonalize the conflict, and put student choice into the equation. In offering students choice, keep the following in mind.

- Make sure you can live with either choice you provide.
- Don't make a negative choice more appealing (for example, avoid, "You can either get started or continue to visit with your friends").
- Be careful about injecting emotions into a choice (for example, avoid, "Get out of the classroom or get to work").

Normally in confrontations, provide students with the choices, and then let them choose. If you teach students choice and decision making as a part of your classroom expectations, they may become skilled in making their own decisions in other situations in and out of school. For example, if two students are in conflict, you might say, "How would you two like to solve this issue?" This allows students the opportunity to come up with a solution. This sort of choice takes much more skill on the part of the students but also has great benefits since they are constructing the solution themselves. We have seen students gain confidence over time when they learn they can actually solve problems and make decisions on their own.

Avoid Power Struggles

Whenever possible, try to avoid power struggles with students. This is especially important when working successfully with trauma-impacted students who may spend a lot of time in power struggles with adults. These same students acted out at school in order to feel some control. Even though they couldn't change their home situation, they were able to control a situation at school as a result of acting out. Model appropriate behaviors for students since they might not be seeing them at home.

Let's see how Ms. Able handles a power struggle with Myrna, the student we discussed earlier in the chapter.

> *One afternoon in mathematics class, Ms. Able asks students working in small groups to solve several problems. As she approaches one group, she notices that Myrna seems upset. She makes an "Are you OK?" gesture toward Myrna but doesn't get a response. Ms. Able decides to watch the group carefully as she circulates around the classroom.*

Ms. Able can see that Myrna appears to be getting more frustrated in working with her group members. She stands by the group and whispers to Myrna, "Are you OK?" Again, Myrna does not acknowledge the question. All of a sudden, Myrna pushes her chair away from the table and exclaims to her group, "All right, do it your way!" Ms. Able asks Myrna if she needs to move to the reflection area of the classroom. Myrna says, "No, they just need to leave me alone!" Ms. Able can see that Myrna needs some time to get centered again, so she can return to the small group.

Rather than get in a power struggle and try to make Myrna move, Ms. Able sends the other group members to the quiet area and has Myrna stay to talk to her. Ms. Able starts the conversation by taking a few deep breaths, then asks Myrna to do the same. After Myrna calms down, Ms. Able asks her to tell her what happened. Once the cause of the situation is clear, Ms. Able and Myrna talk about strategies to use in the future to address similar situations. Finally, Ms. Able brings the rest of the group back to discuss the situation and how they all can avoid problems in the future.

This example shows how Ms. Able reacts to Myrna's disruption. It would have been easy for her to get into a power struggle and try to make Myrna conform to the rules of the classroom. In this case, since Myrna is emotionally out of sorts and not operating in her thinking brain, confrontation or a power struggle will not go well and may even cause other unanticipated consequences. Ms. Able keeps her goal in mind to help Myrna refocus and return to productive work with her group. This helps her stay on track even though the emotions could have escalated. She helps Myrna get her brain regulated and in order again.

When working with trauma-impacted students, and with all students, it's important to keep the objective for student behavior in mind. In most cases, it would be good if the student stopped what he or she was doing and got back on track. The more you can help students be *in control* of getting back on track, the better the situation will be for everyone.

In some situations, when a teacher "digs in" and tries to show the student or the rest of the class who's boss, the harder it seems for the teacher to solve or de-escalate the situation. Trauma-impacted students may not be in control of their own personal situations so helping them to assume more control may take time and patience. Since trauma-impacted students may have learned (and practiced) the fight, flight, hide, freeze, or appease behaviors quite well, you can't overpower them and win in difficult situations by using domineering behaviors. Here some strategies we have found helpful that you can consider using to redirect students while avoiding getting into power struggles.

- **Temporary suspension of opinion:** We introduced this skill earlier in the book. Temporary suspension can be very valuable in working with students that have escalated emotions. The general idea is to listen more intently while using self-talk to avoid taking the student behaviors or comments personally. After students share something with you, it's important to acknowledge what they said by paraphrasing it.
- **Broken record:** In the broken record strategy, the teacher repeats a request or direction but does not engage in an argument with the student. For example, in a situation in which the teacher asks the student to take out his or her textbook, and the student refused, the teacher might restate the expectations until the student complies. The teacher does this without becoming emotional, begging, or increasing the demand. Because the teacher tries to remove the emotion, the student gets no reaction from the teacher and eventually complies.
- **To you, to me:** Teachers can use this verbal strategy to reinforce the importance of his or her request to the class. For example, a student responds to a request by saying, "This is dumb." The teacher could say, "To you, it's dumb; to me, it's important that you are ready to learn." As with the other strategies in this chapter, it's important to try to keep your emotions out of the conversation.
- **Acknowledge students' feelings:** With this strategy, teachers paraphrase or reflect on what they sense are the student's emotions. By sharing they understand (or seem to understand) the student's emotions, they demonstrate that they are trying to see his or her perspective. Understanding does not mean allowing students to misbehave, however. For example, if a teacher makes a request and the student responds with, "This is dumb" and seems frustrated, the teacher could say, "It looks like you are frustrated. I understand, but I still need you to take out your work." As with the other strategies

we've discussed, it's important to move forward without escalating the situation. Try to keep your own emotions in check.

- **Refuse to fight:** At times, students may try to draw teachers into a power struggle by starting a fight. Trauma-impacted students may do this as a way to gain control over the situation. If you refuse to fight or argue, you avoid getting into a losing power struggle. It's hard to not take these attempts personally, but if you keep reminding yourself that the misbehavior may not be based on you, it helps you to stay calm during confrontations.
- **Acknowledge students' power:** This strategy is something that may seem dangerous at first, but students already know they hold some power in the classroom. For example, they can refuse to move or comply with your request. Acknowledging this power may actually make the situation less emotional. In acknowledging this power, you still want to be confident and in charge, but saying something like, "I know you can decide to do this or not, but I know you'll make the right choice and move forward," or "I understand you will make the final decision, but I know you'll make the right choice." Let students know they have power but you have confidence in them.
- **Stop statements:** Sometimes emotions can get out of control, and it seems like an endless confrontation will continue if something or someone doesn't intervene. You may find success in calling a time-out or just saying, "Let's stop and regroup." If you use this strategy, make sure to use nonverbal communication as well, such as a *stop* hand gesture (palm facing forward) or stopping in place and looking at the student. Sometimes, because of the emotion already invested in the conversation, you may need to pair the stop statement with the broken record strategy (repeating the stop direction) until the situation improves. You may even need to walk away while the student argues. Eventually the student will calm down if you don't continue the interaction.

These strategies have worked for us and the educators we have supported over the years. If you choose to try them, make sure you revise and interpret them in a way that is comfortable for you and appropriate for your classroom. Some ideas may work right away, while others may take time and adjustments. There is no magic potion or wand you can wave over a challenging situation to make it better. By thinking about possible strategies in advance, you can prepare yourself for incidents that may arise in your classroom. By being proactive, you can manage potential situations before they become major problems.

Manage Severe and Potentially Dangerous Situations

No matter how calm you are or how carefully you plan, you will encounter difficult situations in the classroom, emotional outbursts, open defiance, and a variety of severe or potentially dangerous behaviors. Some of these situations may be caused by something outside your control, like a problem a student is having at home. Others may be caused by something in your classroom, like a learning task that's too difficult, a comment made by another student, an uncomfortable learning situation (for instance, being placed in a group with a student he or she doesn't like), or one of many other factors. The interventions you choose to use to address severe misbehaviors should be focused on de-escalating the situation and ensuring the safety of all, including the student demonstrating the behavior.

Teachers can use some of the strategies and interventions highlighted earlier in this chapter to de-escalate and manage severe and potentially dangerous situations. Some other strategies to consider include the following.

- Moving on from the situation temporarily in order to let emotions calm, and then coming back and addressing it later
- Asking the rest of the students to leave the classroom while you deal with the disruptive student
- Using an intervention team of colleagues to come to your classroom to help you with the situation
- Creating a private signal that you can use to call the office for assistance in de-escalating the situation

While most teachers like to address the situation as soon as possible and get things back on track, their first priority should be the safety of *all* students in the classroom. If teachers know that a particular behavior or event may cause a potentially dangerous or severe reaction from a student, the best approach is to try to proactively prevent that event from happening in the first place.

Let's look at the following scenario in which a teacher, Mr. Cabrero, intervenes with a student to de-escalate a confrontational situation that could easily get out of control.

> *As he begins his tenth-grade history class, Mr. Cabrero notices that one of his students, Rhonda, appears to be very stressed. She is having trouble sitting still, looking around the room erratically, and clearly not engaged in the lesson. When her classmate, Jason, glances over at her and smirks noticeably, Rhonda stands up and tips over her desk toward him and yells, "Stop looking at me!" Rhonda has exhibited aggressive behavior several times before, so Mr. Cabrero knows he has to do something fast before this situation gets further out of control.*
>
> *Mr. Cabrero calmly speaks to Rhonda while slowly walking toward her desk. He asks her to pick up her desk and books. Even though Rhonda is still upset, Mr. Cabrero calmly repeats his request. After several requests, Rhonda settles down and picks up her desk and books. Mr. Cabrero tells both Rhonda and Jason that he wants to talk with them later in the class period.*
>
> *Toward to the end of the period, Mr. Cabrero meets with both students to find out what happened. He decides that Jason's behavior was just a trigger to Rhonda's behavior, so he talks to Rhonda in more depth to understand what happened. He asks open-ended questions to help Rhonda to identify what caused her to get upset. Mr. Cabrero finds out that Rhonda visited her mom in prison over the weekend, and that upset her. He works with Rhonda to help her to process the situation and sets up an appointment for her to meet with the school counselor for further support. Mr. Cabrero asks the counselor to help Rhonda identify strategies she could use the next time Jason or any other student tries to provoke her. Mr. Cabrero also works with Jason to help him understand how his behaviors are upsetting Rhonda and disrupting the class.*

In this scenario, Mr. Cabrero reacts to Rhonda's outburst without escalating the situation. He needs to move toward the situation while not being too confrontational in addressing it. By getting things under control, then dealing with the outburst later, he let Rhonda get her emotions under control before trying to find out what may have caused the situation.

Sporleder and Forbes (2016) emphasize how influencing a student to change his or her behavior is more effective than dominance, stating, "Ironically, real power and control come from your influence with a child, not through your dominance over a child" (p. 99).

Sporleder and Forbes (2016) approach misbehavior as deregulation in the student's brain. In chapter 1 (page 13), we examined what happens to the brain under stress or attack. In severe situations, the student who is out of control is dealing with a deregulated brain. After the stressful or anxious situation passes, the student can process it and develop alternative strategies to employ in the future (Sporleder & Forbes, 2016).

Childhood trauma can prompt many reactions in students at school, such as emotional outbursts, aggression toward others, fighting with others, and so on. Teachers must deal with these kinds of behaviors immediately, as they could be harmful to the student and others in the classroom. Addressing this issue with parents and families is crucial for future success.

As we will describe in more detail in chapter 6 (page 105), it's important to avoid judgment and unsolicited advice when addressing issues with students' parents and families. In many cases, the trauma the student is experiencing is caused by the behavior of someone in the home. Therefore, if you jump to judgment too quickly, the parent or guardian may put up a wall and withdraw from the relationship. If this happens, the behavior will go underground, making it even more difficult to reach out for help. We are not saying that you should ignore issues of abuse or neglect to develop relationships with parents and families. When you see signs of abuse or neglect, you must report those in compliance with the laws of your state or province.

Richard E. Tremblay (1999) emphasizes that left unchecked, childhood aggression has a debilitating effect on a student's capacity to graduate from high school. In fact, students exhibiting chronic aggression in the first grade only have a 30 percent chance of becoming high school graduates. A Duke University study (2017) claims that "Children who have been victims of violence are more likely to drop out of high school before graduation than their peers." Parents and educators need to work together to mitigate the impact of aggressive behavior (Tremblay, 1999).

Research suggests that when students find their school environment to be supportive and caring, and their parents are engaged in their school lives, they are less likely to become involved in substance abuse, violence, and other problem behaviors (Hawkins, Catalano, Kosterman, Abbott, & Hill, 1999).

The information in this section is designed to give you a brief introduction to managing severe behaviors. For more ideas, please see *Designing Effective Classroom Management* by Jason E. Harlacher (2015).

Conclusion

In this chapter, we have focused on techniques and strategies you can use to manage trauma-impacted students and make your learning environment better for all students in your classroom. Most of these strategies involve trying to remove emotion from the situations and focus on the behaviors rather than the students. As with the other ideas you'll find in this book, you'll need to assess them to see how they fit into your teaching style, meet the needs of your students, and achieve the overall objectives for your classroom climate and culture.

As you continue to learn more about your students and the situations impacting them outside of your classroom, you'll be more comfortable and confident in implementing trauma-informed classroom management strategies. Once you start implementing these strategies, you will notice a difference in how all students, not just those experiencing trauma, become more engaged and focused on classroom activities.

In chapter 6 (page 105), we explore strategies for connecting positively with the families of trauma-impacted students. It's important not to judge these families or try to "fix" them as you develop relationships. Many of these families experience judgment from others, so they aren't interested in your opinion about what they need to change. If families know that you have their children's best interest at heart, you have a much better chance of developing a trusting relationship and working with them to help their children succeed. As you'll see, relationships are one of the foundations for success with trauma-impacted students and families.

QUESTIONS FOR ***Reflection***

As you think about what you learned in this chapter and how it can be implemented in your classroom, reflect on the following questions.

- Why is it important to consider students' learning needs and your own teaching needs when planning classroom management strategies and expectations for learners?
- How can having students assist you in setting up classroom expectations and processes help you manage your classroom?
- How could you use temporary suspension of opinion to help de-escalate a student's behavior before it becomes severe or dangerous? How might acknowledging a student's power help prevent a situation from getting out of hand, more severe, or potentially dangerous?
- How will you use what you learned in this chapter in your own classroom to work with trauma-impacted students and improve their learning environment?

chapter six

Parent and Family Engagement

Toby, a second-grade student, is disruptive in class on average of three days per week. Mr. Cardoza, Toby's teacher, suspects that Toby lives in a very chaotic home and experiences trauma there. Toby's mom, Ginger, is divorced and has several boyfriends who regularly spend the night. In speaking with Toby about the situation, Mr. Cardoza discovers that Ginger is drunk a lot and fights with her boyfriends in front of Toby. Toby has to get up on his own and get ready for school. Mr. Cardoza knows how important it is to provide a safe and accepting environment for Toby at school, but he also knows that it will be helpful to Toby's success if he's able to build a positive relationship with Ginger. Mr. Cardoza will look for any way he can to begin connecting with Ginger and show her he is interested in helping Toby be successful.

Many of you can probably relate to this example from your own classroom experiences. You may be working with students who come from homes like Toby's. Families in trauma are especially in need of positive and nonjudgmental relationships. It's important to find ways to connect with them to build these relationships in order to help their children succeed.

Growing up in traumatic conditions ourselves, we experienced how parent-school relationships can be powerful. As children, living in trauma made us want to blend in and not be noticed, but those teachers who were able to forge positive relationships with our families seemed to know us better and understand our home situations. This knowledge, used in a nonjudgmental way, helped them work in partnership with our families. Even though these teachers weren't able to change our home lives, just knowing that they understood some of what we were going through made us feel more connected and committed to them.

One of John's teachers built a positive relationship with his father. John's father felt comfortable working with this teacher and saw him as invested in John's success. This teacher was a positive influence in John's life.

Just reaching out to build relationships with families of students in trauma can make a difference in their lives. You can't always change their home situations, but you can gain an understanding of what students may be experiencing and provide a positive environment in your classroom.

In this chapter, we focus on building relationships with and engaging parents and families of trauma-impacted students. As you review the information in this chapter, be sure to focus on the following.

- The importance of building relationships with parents and families of students in trauma
- The differences between parent and family involvement and parent and family engagement
- How to build positive, nonjudgment relationships with parents and families
- Various factors that affect parent and family engagement in school, such as educational and cultural backgrounds
- Strategies for increasing parent and family engagement

The Importance of Parent and Family Engagement

There is widespread debate in education about what constitutes the most accurate predictor of academic achievement. The reality is that it's not socioeconomic status nor how prestigious the school a child attends. The best predictor of student success in school is the extent to which parents and families encourage and support learning at home and get involved in their children's education (National Parent Teacher Association, 2000; Waterford.org, 2018).

In developing this chapter, Tom was reminded of a Pauline B. Gough (1991) quote that drove his initial interest in ensuring deep, meaningful parent engagement.

"Educating the child without the support and encouragement of the home is akin to raking leaves in a high wind" (p. 339). The image of raking leaves against the wind, thinking you're making progress only to turn around and see the lawn still covered with leaves in spite of your hard efforts, is like working alone or even against parents. Raking with the wind is akin to working *with* parents. When parents are engaged in their children's lives at school, students know they have the home support and knowledge they need to not only finish their work but also to apply that skill as they continue to develop a lifelong love of learning. In traumatic home situations, the "high wind" of damaging chaos can be very strong and difficult to overcome. Building relationships with these families may help to calm these winds.

After an analysis of numerous studies on parent engagement, educational researchers Nancy E. Hill and Diana F. Tyson (2009) conclude that there is a connection between family engagement and academic achievement. The sooner educators establish parent engagement, the more effective they are in increasing student performance. Not surprisingly, Eric Dearing, Holly Kreider, Sandra Simpkins, and Heather B. Weiss (2006) suggest that parent partnerships formed during elementary school years build a strong foundation for student success and future engagement opportunities. The earlier they engage, and the more committed parents remain, the better the outcomes for all students.

Building strong relationships and engaging with the families of trauma-impacted students can help these students see teachers as adults they can trust. As a teacher, you can work with your colleagues to develop a consistent state of engagement. This objective can be the focus of the entire school staff.

Students with engaged parents are more likely to:

- Earn higher grades or test scores (American Psychological Association, 2014a)
- Graduate from high school and attend postsecondary education (Grand Rapids Public School District, n.d.)
- Develop self-confidence and motivation in the classroom (Wairimu, Macharia, & Muiru, 2016)
- Possess better social skills and exhibit improved classroom behavior (Waterford.org, 2018)

They are also less likely to:

- Have low self-esteem (Waterford.org, 2018)
- Need redirection in the classroom (Sheldon & Jung, 2015)
- Develop behavioral issues (Waterford.org, 2018)

According to Waterford.org (2018), "Parent engagement also decreases chronic absenteeism, or missing more than twenty days of a school year." Absenteeism is a significant challenge, particularly in remote communities, and can be mitigated by engaging parents in these school communities. As an example, Steven B. Sheldon and Sol Bee Jung (2015) determined that when teachers engaged with parents through home visits, student absences dropped by 20 percent. According to Sheldon and Joyce L. Epstein (2004), this was true even after accounting for grade level and previous absences. Students with engaged parents report fewer days of school missed overall.

Before offering methods and strategies for building deep and trusting relationships with parents and families and engaging them with their children's education, it's important to discuss the differences between parent and family involvement and engagement.

Differences Between Parent and Family Involvement and Engagement

It's important to delineate the difference between what we refer to as parent and family *engagement* from what is often seen in schools—parent and family *involvement*. We can define *involvement* as "to enfold or envelop" ("Involvement," n.d.); we can define *engagement* as "to interlock with; to mesh" ("Engagement," n.d.).

Parent engagement differs from parent involvement, though both are valuable. Waterford.org (2018) states:

> Parent involvement is when parents participate in school events or activities, and teachers provide learning resources or information about their student's grades. Unlike in parent engagement, teachers hold the primary responsibility to set educational goals. They relate to parents not as a partner but an advisor who guides them through academic support for their child.

This is an important concept for working with students in trauma. When you engage with parents, ask for their advice rather than ask them to do things they might not be comfortable with or have the skills to do. This advisory role may be different for each parent, depending on his or her interest and ability.

When parents are engaged, they make a commitment to work together in collaboration with the school. According to Waterford.org (2018), "Parents commit to prioritizing their child's educational goals, and teachers commit to listening and providing a space for collaboration with parents." *Collaboration* also means that all parties (parents and teachers) work together and share responsibility for the success of their children.

Let's look at the difference between involvement and engagement through a variety of lenses. As you review these differences in figure 6.1 (page 110), keep the perspective of a parent in trauma in mind.

According to Waterford.org (2018):

> It helps to think of parent involvement as the first step to parent engagement. While teachers can advise parents on some things, parents also have important information about their child that teachers might not know. Both can bring perspectives to the table that enrich a student's learning experience. Neither is complete without the other.

As Larry Ferlazzo (2011) notes:

> A school striving for family involvement often leads with its mouth—identifying projects, needs, and goals and then telling parents how they can contribute. A school striving for parent engagement, on the other hand, tends to lead with its ears—listening to what parents think, dream, and worry about. (p. 11)

After the Every Student Succeeds Act (ESSA) replaced No Child Left Behind (NCLB), the focus for educators needed to shift from parent involvement to engagement. Teachers used to involve parents by giving them resources, inviting them to activities, and helping them monitor their children's progress. Now you must partner with parents to set goals for their children and find ways to strengthen your classroom. When you engage parents in the learning process, your school community is richer for it, and student outcomes more closely approximate students' abilities (Waterford.org, 2018).

FACTOR	INVOLVEMENT	ENGAGEMENT
Who Initiates?	When parents are involved, they act on the ideas of others, largely the school administration, and are basically a "rubber stamp" to approve direction. Some parents in traumatic situations have been mandated to be involved with the school.	When parents are engaged, they feel welcomed by the school administration to directly offer ideas and suggestions based on the information that is openly shared with them. The administration addresses their needs authentically. These engagement behaviors focus on helping their child.
Is This an Invitation or an Expectation?	When you involve parents, you have them do your bidding and take actions that the staff might see as important.	When you engage parents, you support the ideas they have suggested and provide more information to complete the picture they might have. This is when it's important to help them see that you have their child's best interests in mind.
Roles of Parents and Staff	When you involve parents, you use them as figureheads for the school agenda.	When you engage parents, you support their plans and assist where you can. Engaging them in activities in which they feel comfortable and confident builds the relationship.
Purpose	When you involve parents, you remind them of what you are already doing and how they can support those programs.	When you engage parents, you are open to new approaches that contribute not only to the life of the school but also to the community at large.

Source: Adapted from Ferlazzo, 2011.

Figure 6.1: Differences between parent and family involvement and engagement.

"Two-way communication between parents and teachers [in engaged relationships] commits students to daily attendance and raises class participation levels" (Waterford.org, 2018), while also giving parents the sense of being members of the school community. Tom's own personal experience when he first entered school leadership validates this belief, as he led a school that went from the proverbial rock bottom (and undesirable to potential educators or families) to a school of impact (with educators and parents transferring in due to its success).

Figure 6.2 summarizes the discussion about parent and family involvement versus engagement.

Involvement	Engagement
Our agenda (owned by the school)	Our agenda (owned by parents)
Top down	Side by side
One way	Back and forth
School's power	Shared power
Teacher knowledge	Teacher and parent knowledge
Fundraising and advocacy	Teaching and learning

Figure 6.2: Parent and family involvement or engagement?

In this model of communication and authentic engagement, teachers also benefit. They can work with parents to help with home study on key concepts. Authentically "engaged parents tend to think more highly of teachers, which improve s teacher morale. Knowing more about a student's family life can also help teachers prepare lessons that better fit that student's needs or interact more efficiently with families" (Waterford.org, 2018). Research from Anne T. Henderson and Nancy Berla (1994) suggests that classrooms with engaged parents perform better as a whole. As educators with decades of experience, we believe that the larger the team supporting student success, the greater the likelihood of success.

In developing a positive relationship with parents of students in trauma, it's important to consider how to approach parents and families gently and build the relationship in steps. You might think of scaffolding the relationship to establish a foundation of comfort that you may then build on.

We introduced Toby and his mother Ginger earlier in the chapter. Now, let's see how building a relationship helps Mr. Cardoza work toward parent engagement with Ginger.

> *In his conversations with teachers who have had Toby in the past, Mr. Cardoza learns that most of the previous interactions teachers have had with Ginger have been to report negative behaviors. He wants to break this cycle and start to build a positive relationship with her. He decides to reach out to Ginger after the first positive*

behavior Toby exhibits in his classroom. Toby is fond of the class pet rabbit, Jack, and volunteers to care for him. One afternoon when Ginger picks up Toby after school, Mr. Cardoza greets her then tells her how helpful Toby has been with the rabbit.

When Mr. Cardoza delivers the compliment, Ginger acts surprised and says, "Really? Thank you for letting me know." Mr. Cardoza realizes that Ginger may not have heard many positive comments about Toby. He decides to make it a priority to share at least one positive message with Ginger each week. These positive messages must be sincere if he is going to build a relationship with her. As he continues to share the good things Toby does, Mr. Cardoza notices that Ginger seems more comfortable in interacting with him. He has established a foundation for a positive relationship.

In this scenario, Mr. Cardoza works to build a relationship based on Ginger's need for positive information about Toby. He knows that Ginger may never be the type of parent who volunteers in his classroom, but once he builds a positive relationship, he'll be able to engage with her in other productive ways. Since Ginger's behaviors are contributing to Toby's traumatic home life, Mr. Cardoza is developing the relationship slowly to build trust.

Parent involvement in schools is the first step to parent engagement, the ultimate goal of parents as partners. When families and teachers work together to establish a classroom learning community, the effect on students is significant. Students don't just have higher test scores—their attendance, self-esteem, and graduation rates rise too (Waterford.org, 2018). Developing these strong relationships moves beyond being optional—it is the key to helping students, both behaviorally and academically, reach their full potential. If educators don't take advantage of cultivating these important partnerships, they are missing out on a significant way to impact every student's capacity for growth.

As Waterford.org (2018) notes:

> Teachers who focus on [developing] parent [relationships and] engagement often see a profound change in their classrooms. The more parents [become] involved in their children's education, [and the earlier this engagement occurs], the better their entire class's motivation, behavior, and grades become. . . . Encouraging parent engagement is more than common courtesy. It's one of the best ways to create a positive learning environment for

every student. To create a community built on parent-teacher relationships in your school, find out what parent engagement is and how to nurture it.

While building relationships with families in trauma can be challenging (because of a variety of factors, including their interest in keeping their struggles private, their own poor school experiences, and so on), the rewards are great. In many cases, these parents may have an aversion to working with public officials. In their past experiences with teachers or principals, they may have been judged negatively.

So far, we've outlined the importance of building relationships with parents of students in trauma. Once a foundational relationship is formed, you can move forward to develop a more collaborative relationship—parent engagement. Let's see how Mr. Cardoza's developing relationship with Ginger evolved into engaging Ginger in working with Toby.

Since Mr. Cardoza started sharing sincere and positive feedback about Toby, Ginger begins to feel comfortable and trusts him to do what's best for her son. Once this relationship is established, Mr. Cardoza asks Ginger for information about Toby's interests, what she thinks motivates him, and ways to work with him more productively based on her experiences. Mr. Cardoza can't use all her ideas, but the fact that he shows interest in her opinions helps when he encounters problems with Toby and needs her ideas and support. The comfort continues to grow, and Mr. Cardoza is able to engage Ginger in helping him make a positive impact on Toby's learning.

Mr. Cardoza finds out that it takes time to build trust to get to the level of parent engagement with Ginger, but the payoff in Toby's success is clear. In conversations to help develop the relationship, Mr. Cardoza learns that Ginger was also raised in a home with trauma. This helps him understand her response when interactions become challenging or emotional. While the relationship doesn't change the situation at home, it helps both Ginger and Toby understand that Mr. Cardoza and the school are invested in their success.

As you explore the strategies in the next section, think about how you can customize some of them to match the strengths of the parents you wish to engage in your classroom.

Helping parents feel comfortable engaging at home and working in collaboration with teachers requires a strong relationship involving trust and support. Let's look at this aspect of relationships.

A Foundation of Trust and Support

In *Thriving as a New Teacher*, Eller and Eller (2016) discuss the importance of developing relationships with families. When working with families of students who are experiencing trauma, it's important to develop supportive relationships because many of these parents are not normally active in the school community.

In our own experiences living with trauma, our families did not naturally trust authority figures such as teachers. These authority figures could report our families to law enforcement and social services who could take action to penalize them. There was a natural inclination to cover up or hide the situations.

Just as our own families did, other families in trauma often have the same fear of being judged (and suffering consequences) for their home situations. Because of the natural mistrust that might occur, it's important for educators to try to build trusting relationships with families of students in trauma. These initial relationships need to be built on nonjudgmental and trusting actions.

Following are some general strategies to consider for building the foundation of trust needed to develop positive and productive relationships with families of trauma-impacted students.

Avoid Judgment

It's easy to look at other people's situations through your own lenses and pass judgment. Withholding judgment is important in working with any parent but especially when working with parents and families of students in trauma. We have found that while they might need help, support, or advice to move out of their situation, your ideas and maybe even your support may not be welcome until you've developed a trusting relationship with them. Accepting people as they are can be hard to do, but in the end, you'll be able to make a larger impact than if you judge them or give advice too early in the relationship.

We're not suggesting that you ignore dangerous or potentially life-threatening situations. In most places, educators are all mandatory reporters for students who are being abused. In these cases, developing a relationship comes secondary to protecting a child. In most jurisdictions, there is a statutory requirement to report any sign of abuse or disclosure that indicates abuse. There is no leeway nor consideration of fracturing a relationship with the family. It's a legal requirement.

Listen First, Talk Later

In verbal communications, it pays to listen more than talk, especially early in a relationship. Using skills such as active listening and paraphrasing can help to build trust in a relationship. Putting your own thoughts and ideas on hold and truly listening to what parents have to say goes a long way to building relationships and engagement. For example, if a parent is telling you a story about an issue in the neighborhood, it's better to listen instead of stopping the story to share your advice for how they should address the problem.

Control Negative Reactions

When working with families in trauma, you may learn some information that will surprise or shock you. When hearing shocking news, negative reactions and facial expressions can communicate judgment. Since nonverbal communication makes up a large part of the message in a conversation, minimizing them will make it appear that you are not judgmental.

If possible, when talking with parents, try to control your reactions to surprising news. This can be hard to do, but if you prepare yourself in advance, you may not act (or look) as shocked or surprised as you are. Framing your thoughts in advance and telling yourself to watch your reactions can help you avoid looking surprised or shocked.

Focus on Students and Their Families

Parents will usually be more motivated to build a relationship with you if you are able to focus on doing what's best for their children. Because they fear you might judge them as people or parents, you should continually frame your actions around the needs of their children. In working with Toby's mom, Mr. Cardoza put his focus on Toby. That focus helped Ginger to feel more relaxed in working with Mr. Cardoza. None of his efforts to build a relationship with Ginger were based on judging her or her home situation. When parents know teachers have the support and success of their child as their first priority, parents are much more willing to engage in a relationship with them.

Similarly, focus on family needs to provide a foundation for your relationship efforts. If you strive to build relationships based on what's good or helpful for *them*, you'll have more success. How can you determine parent or family needs?

Do a survey to gauge their interest in learning more about your school, school policies, parenting skills, or child development. Then work with them to develop family or parent education programs based on your survey results. These opportunities could focus on topics such as understanding report cards and assessments, parent-teacher conferences, and home support, or family-related topics such as child development, discipline, or community support services (Michigan Department of Education, 2015).

Be Aware of Family Cultures

The Michigan Department of Education (2015) notes that "in many countries and cultures, there is a belief that the teacher's responsibility is to educate a student while he or she is at school; the parent is responsible for the education at home" (p. 77). This may lead some of immigrant families to show their respect for schools and educators by keeping their distance. Schools need to be diligent about breaking through this barrier. Parents may feel uncomfortable or unwelcome in their child's school if there is a lack of cultural awareness and diversity that they can relate to.

Ensure that your classroom is welcoming and family friendly—whatever a student's particular family may look like. Post signs in multiple languages that are reflective of your population, and decorate your room and adjoining hallways with works of art and flags of countries represented in your community. Attend cultural events, as parents and community members enjoy seeing educators outside the school setting involved in the community. The American Psychological Association (2003) also offers some guidelines on multicultural education and training.

As the demographics of the typical student in schools change across the United States (see figure 6.3), so too should schools be aware that parents' backgrounds might influence their view toward school and their role within it.

According to the National Center for Education Statistics (2018):

> Since fall 2014, less than half of public school students have been White. The percentage of public school students who are White, along with the percentage of students who are American Indian/Alaska Native, is projected to continue to decline . . . through at least fall 2029. The percentages of students who are Asian and of two or more races are projected to increase. The percentages of Black, Hispanic, and Pacific Islander students are expected to be about the same in 2029 as they were in 2017.

According to the National Center for Education Statistics (2018), the projected 50.7 million U.S. public school students entering prekindergarten through grade 12 in fall 2020 are expected to include:

- 23.4 million White students
- 14.0 million Hispanic students
- 7.6 million Black students
- 2.8 million Asian students
- 2.3 million students of two or more races
- 0.5 million American Indian/Alaska Native students
- 0.2 million Pacific Islander students

Source: National Center for Education Statistics, 2018.

Figure 6.3: Changing student and family demographics.

B. Hudnall Stamm and Matthew J. Friedman (2000) find that there are significant differences in the way societies view and treat survivors of adversity. The National Child Traumatic Stress Network (2017a) identifies six steps for educators to consider as they deal with race and trauma.

1. Learn about the impacts of history and systemic racism.
2. Create and support safe and brave environments.
3. Model and support honesty and authenticity.
4. Honor the impacts of history and systemic racism.
5. Encourage and empower students as leaders.
6. Care for yourself.

Understanding race and trauma and the effects the interchange between those two factors have on students in the classroom through these six steps will help educators to bridge the gap as they become more culturally and trauma sensitive.

This information does not mean the fundamental operation of schools needs to change. However, the responses to trauma might need to be different based on the cultural background or ethnicity of students and their families. As schools move along the continuum of becoming more trauma responsive, all available factors must be considered.

Understand Family Educational Experiences

When attempting to build relationships with parents and families, learn about and be aware of their education levels. Parents of students in trauma may not have graduated from high school as a result of their own traumatic experiences. Parents with education levels lower than yours may feel intimidated in talking with you or could even be resentful of your education level. Try to relate to them as people, without judgement, and be careful not to let your education level get in the way of developing a sound relationship.

Some parents of students in trauma may have experienced trauma themselves and had poor school experiences. They might think their voice is of little consequence and may feel out of place attending meetings with other parents. By reaching out to parents and families, educators help them see that what the school is offering is different than the experiences they had when they were in school.

It's important that educators provide parents with the opportunity to view school in a positive light. Actively listening to parents' questions and concerns and treating these concerns seriously, rather than explaining them away, indicates to parents they are part of the team ensuring success for all students. If background experiences include traumatic events, the parent may become a resource for others or may benefit from the supports the school puts in place.

The NASP School Safety and Crisis Response Committee (2015) offers the following suggestions:

- Recognize and be sensitive to the fact that problem behaviors can be the manifestation of trauma-related anxiety
- Help children manage their feelings by teaching and modeling effective coping strategies
- Promote family activities to bring them closer to the ones they love
- Watch for changes in behaviors
- Respond calmly and compassionately, but without displaying shock or judgment
- Anticipate challenging times or situations that may be reminders of the [trauma], and provide additional support

Avoid Educational Jargon or Codes

Educators often use jargon with which parents may be unfamiliar. This jargon or code is clear to educators but not to parents. The jargon in a conversation may sound like this: "Hello, Mr. Smith. Our guiding coalition met to look at our latest CFA, and we are proposing that your child receive additional Tier 2 RTI support." This language, which may be common in K–12 education, could seem like insiders' code to students' parents, and thus inhibits their ability to understand and engage in their child's education. When working with parents, be sure to always define terms and explain their significance for their child. Being clear and simple can go a long way in helping you develop a good relationship with parents.

Use a Variety of Communication Methods

Traditionally, teachers have been able to build relationships through face-to-face or verbal methods. In the modern, technological world, they may need to use others. According to a Blackboard (2016) paper. "Trends in Community Engagement: How K–12 Schools Are Meeting the Expectations of Parents for Digital Communications," there is an emerging form of communication that some schools have been slow to respond to. Blackboard (2016) also reveals that:

- 87 percent of parents indicated [in 2016] that a personal email was the most effective vehicle for communicating with them, an increase of 36 percent since 2010.
- 55 percent of parents would like their child's teacher or school to simply "text them" when they want to communicate information. In 2010, text messaging was the preference of only five percent of parents.
- Only 50 percent of the parents noted that a face-to-face meeting was the most effective way to communicate information to them, a significant decrease from [2015] when 64 percent of parents valued the type of communications approach.
- Only 48 percent of parents chose a personal phone call as the most effective way to communicate information to them.
- Parents of elementary students who are under 40 years of age themselves are the most supportive of the use of emerging digital tools to support school-to-home communications.

We don't suggest that schools abandon all other forms of communication, including many traditional methods. This information does indicate, however, that educators need to explore additional options to engage parents in ways that suit them. While exploring ways to ensure parents can become fully engaged in their child's education, it's important to recognize that sometimes there are additional challenges that may work against your best efforts. The following section identifies some of these significant barriers as well as some options for overcoming the barriers.

Factors Impacting Parent and Family Engagement

As previously noted, *parent engagement* can be thought of as "parents and teachers sharing a responsibility to help their children learn and meet educational goals" (Waterford.org, 2018). Even though we have been talking about developing relationships with parents of students experiencing trauma, you'll want to think about how you can develop relationships with *all* your students' parents or guardians. Parent and family engagement in education matters now more than ever for all students but is especially important for trauma-impacted students. According to a report by the National Child Traumatic Stress Network (2017b), "Evidence-based practices for children exposed to trauma frequently involve treatment for both the child and their primary caregivers. Research has identified that involving caregivers in treatment services significantly increases the likelihood of positive outcomes for children."

There are a myriad of factors driving this change in the capacity for parents and families to become engaged with their child's school. Leading the list is the change in economic pressures affecting most families. These same economic pressures can contribute to childhood trauma. It is a significant challenge to make ends meet with only one income to pay the bills. In homes where both adults are working, this leaves precious little time at the end of the day to engage with schools. The Organisation for Economic Co-operation and Development (2020) notes, "Lower levels of parental engagement may be influenced by pressures derived from economic and social difficulties, lack of flexible work hours, extremely long work hours and single parenting."

Getting dinner on the table and having a bit of quality time supersede attending a school event. Other parents might have scheduling or transportation issues that make volunteering or attending parent-teacher conferences challenging.

With low-income or minority families, there could be some discomfort or a lack of cultural awareness on the part of the school (Michigan Department of Education, 2015).

It's critical that educators reach out early and often to build connections with parents. If parent-teacher relationships aren't established early in the year, parents may feel they are not welcome at school. When educators engage parents early and, hopefully, before a major problem occurs, then at the first indication of a concern, educators and parents can work together to solve the problem before it becomes a full-blown issue. As we saw in the earlier scenario, Mr. Cardoza reaches out to Ginger early in the year to build the relationship before Toby gets into trouble. Now, if issues arise, Mr. Cardoza can use the positive relationship that they have developed to work together on the issues.

Research from Blackboard (2016) heightens this concern, as it shows a decline in parents who believe that face-to-face, intimate parent-teacher communication is effective. Waterford.org (2018) states, "Parents now prefer remote methods of communication, like online student portals, and they are less likely to attend parent-teacher conferences or school activities." This should raise a red flag for schools as to what *parent engagement* actually means. We are not opposed to using digital tools to help families stay informed of student progress on academic outcomes or attendance. However, we believe it's a poor substitute for authentic engagement and that students miss out when parents don't offer their time and support to their school communities. Families in trauma may have fewer resources and less ability to communicate via email or even over the phone. Educators must look at various options for reaching out to these parents and families in ways that work for them.

Educators must also recognize that challenges can become more prevalent for some groups. Research from Child Trends (2018) suggests that parent and family involvement is lowest in families below the poverty line, families with older children, families who do not speak the primary language of the community or region, and parents who did not graduate high school. Our own anecdotal evidence reminds us that a lack of parent success in school is often a precursor to a lack of parent involvement in their children's school. We discussed the importance of these issues earlier, but it's good to keep them in the forefront of your thoughts as you work to build family relationships.

How to Increase Parent and Family Engagement

While we often hear that parents tend to be more involved in their children's school during elementary school, we maintain that it's never too late to build the foundations for parent-teacher communication in school. Clearly, as with most successful school endeavors, the earlier parents are engaged, the more equipped students will be to benefit from support of their families and reach their academic potential. Tom's eleven years of experience as an administrator of a grades 7–9 middle school reinforced how powerful a force the parents became and how significant they were, not only in the lives of their children but also in the life of the school. The move from involvement to engagement was a key factor in the success of the school. Parents and families took charge of the quarterly awards ceremonies at the school, which resulted in a profound shift in how students were recognized for effort, improvement, deportment, and academic progress. This meant a big increase in the number of students recognized as well as students feeling their efforts contributed to the positive school culture.

Try these parent and family engagement strategies to transform involvement into meaningful parent partnerships.

- Reach out to parents at the beginning of the school year. By talking to parents before you actually work with their children, you'll be able to gain their perspectives and gather important information. Reaching out early helps you develop relationships before you encounter difficulties. With parents of trauma-impacted students, you may need to reach out in more personal ways. For example, having a personal conversation with these parents at the start of the year goes a long way in building successful relationships. That way, when they have questions, they'll feel comfortable reaching out to you.
- Provide multiple opportunities for parents and families to connect with the school. Various forums to engage parents include volunteer shifts during events such as school dances or awards ceremonies, classroom activities such as field trips and sporting events, and parent-teacher committee meetings.

- Share your classroom and school goals or expectations with parents, and ask them to do the same. Let them know what happens when occasional poor judgement from their children occurs.
- Connect with parents on a face-to-face basis as much as possible. In addition to personal communication, use emails, texts, or apps to keep parents up to date on upcoming classroom and school events, and assist (if needed) in creating a parent section in your methods of communication, for example, a column in the school bulletin or space on the school Facebook page.
- Support initiatives by parents that support the work of the school community. For instance, Tom had parents who created their own quarterly system of recognition for students based on their efforts, aligning with the purpose of the school.

Address common challenges that inhibit or prevent parent and family engagement, such as scheduling conflicts with parents' jobs or activities, or an intimidating atmosphere. As the opening narrative to this chapter indicates, parents may have had past negative experiences with school, so they may not easily recognize the positive experiences you and your team are trying to create. Meet parents where they need you to meet them and build from there.

The CDC (2012) proposes the following framework for schools to consider when they are looking to increase parent and family engagement in schools.

1. **Connect** with parents by building positive relationships and communicating the school's vision to work together with parents to guide children's health and learning.
2. **Engage** parents by providing a variety of activities and frequent occasions to fully involve parents including providing parenting support, increasing communication with parents, creating volunteer opportunities, supporting learning at home, encouraging parents to be part of decision making in schools, and collaborating with the community.
3. **Sustain** parent engagement by addressing the common challenges to getting and keeping parents engaged such as scheduling conflicts, transportation, making parents feel welcome in the school, and supporting teachers in building relationships with families.

The CDC (2012) goes on to state that parent engagement in schools is a shared responsibility in which schools commit to reaching out to engage parents in meaningful ways, and parents commit to actively supporting their children's learning and development. This support improves children's learning, development, and health.

Once you have developed a trusting relationship with parents and families, you can gradually start to work with them to help trauma-impacted students develop resilience. You may need to move very slowly at first in order to maintain trust while helping students deal with trauma. Let's see how Mr. Cardoza builds on the trust he is building with Toby's mother, Ginger, about Toby's needs at school and at home. This leads to Ginger letting her guard down and fully engaging with the process.

> *After several weeks of communication with Ginger, Mr. Cardoza feels that he has developed some trust with her. He has developed this trust because he has focused his communication on Toby's best interest and not judged Ginger or the home situation.*
>
> *During their conversations, Mr. Cardoza discovers that Toby is at home by himself for several hours after school while he waits for Ginger to get home from work. Mr. Cardoza knows Toby likes to help out, so he offers Ginger the option of having Toby help take care of some of the classroom pets, assist in the media center, and perform other tasks once per week after school. Ginger can pick him up at school, so she doesn't have to worry about him walking home later than normal.*

In this scenario, Mr. Cardoza provides a way to keep Toby engaged in a positive way, reducing the amount of time he's home alone, and giving himself the opportunity to have informal conversations with Ginger when she picks up Toby after school. As the trust continues to develop, Mr. Cardoza can start giving Ginger ideas for working positively with Toby at home, such as involving him in an organization like Big Brothers, Big Sisters of America (www.bbbs.org).

This level of engagement is possible because of the relationship Mr. Cardoza has developed with Ginger. Early in the relationship, he listened and learned. Later, Ginger trusted him to share ideas. Your relationship with students' parents or guardians may not develop in the same manner. You may not be able to find projects for students to do after school to reduce the time they are alone at home.

However, by continuing to work with families, you may develop a level of trust so you can find ways to collaborate and engage in the best interest of the students.

Keep parents and families engaged by offering some of the following suggestions for how they can assist their children dealing with trauma.

- Establish a predictable structure and schedule to increase their stability.
- Make sure their child has space and time for rest, play, and fun.
- Speak of the future and make plans to help counteract the feeling among traumatized children that the future is frightening, bleak, or unpredictable.
- Reassure their children and place the traumatic situation in context if possible, as children often personalize situations and worry about their own safety even if the traumatic event occurred far away (HelpGuide, n.d.).
- Manage their own stress, remaining calm, relaxed, and focused in an effort to help their children manage theirs.

Conclusion

In this chapter, we examined ideas and strategies to help build positive relationships with parents and families in order to help their children experiencing trauma. In many cases, these parents have had some role in creating the traumatic situation, but in some cases they have not. Once you establish positive relationships, you can move to the next level to involve and engage parents and families. The strategies we outlined in this chapter are designed to help parents of children who have experienced trauma, but they can be used with *all* students' parents.

As you work to help students in your classroom deal with traumatic situations and build the resilience they need to both survive and thrive, developing partnerships with and engaging parents is crucial. Relationship building and engagement takes time, but the time you invest in these relationships greatly benefit students both inside and outside the classroom. This is surely a worthy investment.

QUESTIONS FOR *Reflection*

As you think about what you learned in this chapter and how it can be implemented in your classroom, reflect on the following questions.

- Why is developing positive relationships so important in working productively with parents and families? What are some ways you can build relationships with students' parents and families?
- Why would parents who may have a role in the trauma their child is experiencing be reluctant to work with you? How can you build trust while addressing their child's needs?
- What are the concepts and strategies you learned in this chapter? How can you implement them in your classroom and in your work with parents and families?

Epilogue

When we began drafting this manuscript, terms like *pandemic, remote learning, hybrid learning,* and *Zoom* were infrequently (if ever) part of the conversation in schools and districts, let alone the general population. As this book headed to press, it didn't seem like we could have a conversation about education without regular and frequent mention of those terms (and many others connected to the COVID-19 pandemic).

As we shifted the text to reflect the times, we knew that the essence of trauma-sensitive instruction, the strategies and connections we hope this book has provided, would not change. Responding to the pandemic is likely the single biggest challenge educators will face in their careers. A global occurrence with the potential to disrupt three consecutive school years is not something educators are used to in this profession. The lingering impact will be felt in schools in a myriad of ways, from reinvigorating past traumatic experiences to creating new ones for students and colleagues. Yet, educators do what they always have done—they carry on and continue to educate students to the best of their abilities.

Events like the pandemic can reinvigorate feelings from past traumatic events in our lives. Although individuals may have experienced some healing and growth in the time since they experienced these events, the trauma of the pandemic and the challenges that flow from it may take individuals back to a place of hardship or despair. Clinical psychologist Seth J. Gillihan (2020) writes, "The fear and uncertainty we face from COVID-19 can be a trigger for *any* kind of previous trauma, such as accidents, assaults, or abuse—any horrifying event that you experienced as unpredictable and uncontrollable." A past traumatic event can further inflame a current response resulting in reactions, responses, and the potential for ongoing major life disruptions.

When schools emerge fully and clearly postpandemic, educators should anticipate certain changes. Results from the 2020 First American School District Panel Survey offer some revealing findings, including: "About two in ten districts have already adopted, plan to adopt, or are considering adopting virtual schools as part of their district portfolio after the end of the COVID-19 pandemic" (Schwartz, Grant, Diliberti, Hunter, & Setodji, 2020, p. 1).

The district leaders who provided feedback coalesced around the notion of parent and student demand to see online instruction in various forms continue to be a part of the educational services provided. The authors identify three concerns that were predominant for district leaders going forward (Schwartz, et al., 2020).

1. Disparities in students' opportunities to learn during the COVID-19 pandemic
2. Students' social and emotional learning (SEL) needs
3. Insufficient funding to cover staff

We are not returning to the *old normal*—on many levels that structure does not exist anymore. Neither should we plan for a move forward to the *new normal*, as the use of the word *normal* conveys a connection to something that, based on the survey, might need to shift. Instead, we encourage educators to plan for a move to a *new better*—schools and districts that embrace the best of what educators knew pre-pandemic and incorporate the best of what they have learned during the pandemic. Rather than focusing on the notion of *learning loss,* which seems to be raising anxiety levels (Education Support, 2020; Wong, 2020), educators must address the needs of students with unfinished learning.

While attending to the importance of these events, we do not want to lose sight of the significant impact of trauma that was occurring before the pandemic. If the changes that occur in schools and districts in attending to trauma are forever improved, then some further good will have come from the crisis. We hope there is a renewed interest and heightened awareness of the need for schools and districts to address trauma and its impact with a schoolwide and districtwide approach.

In conclusion, we would like to offer these five reminders as you continue to work and grow as trauma-sensitive educators.

1. **Work together:** A strong, committed team will overcome challenges a talented group of individuals never can. A team, built

on collaboration, becomes an unstoppable force. "As part of the collaborative team, you're either getting better at your job or helping someone else get better" (Williams & Hierck, 2015, p. 53).

2. **Keep a routine:** Research has consistently shown that routines can play an important role in mental health (Arlinghaus & Johnston, 2018). We've heard from many colleagues that during the pandemic, routines have helped keep them grounded and reduced the mental load brought on by needing to make too many decisions.
3. **Keep talking:** An extension of number 1 is to make sure you have a buddy system on staff. Having regular check-ins with colleagues (and committing to checking in regularly) gives you another person to lean on and share the load with. Being part of a trauma-sensitive school means having an open environment where everyone is willing to help everyone, and where educators know that they can talk to other colleagues throughout the school.
4. **Remember the students:** As difficult and challenging as the pandemic has been, always remember your calling. You have been asked to do so much during this time and have shone admirably. Use the tools in this book as touchstones to reconnect to the reason you became an educator in the first place—to make a difference.
5. **Put on your own mask first:** Self-care can't be at the bottom of your to-do list. There's a reason why flight attendants advise you to put on your own oxygen mask first. It's OK to think of self-care as health care and ensure you are healthy and able to take on the role. Equally important—if your own mental wellness is flagging, seek help from a professional. It's not a sign of weakness and will go a long way to ensuring you can be strong in the face of these unprecedented times.

As you work to ensure all students are successful, take stock in your success, continue to provide opportunities for *all* students, and keep the potential impact of trauma in mind. You can and will make a difference and be that transition person helping to build resonance for the many students you serve.

References and Resources

Alisic, E. (2012). Teachers' perspectives on providing support to children after trauma: A qualitative study. *School Psychology Quarterly, 27*(1), 51–59. Accessed at www.apa.org/pubs/journals/features/spq-27-1-51.pdf on December 17, 2020.

American Psychological Association. (2003). Guidelines on multicultural education, training, research, practice, and organizational change for psychologists. *American Psychologist, 58*(5), 377–402.

American Psychological Association. (2014a). *Parent engagement in schools.* Accessed at www.apa.org/pi/lgbt/programs/safe-supportive/parental-engagement/default.aspx on October 20, 2020.

American Psychological Association. (2014b). *The road to resilience.* Accessed at https://uncw.edu/studentaffairs/committees/pdc/documents/the%20road%20to%20resilience.pdf on October 20, 2020.

Arlinghaus, K. R., & Johnston, C. A. (2018). The importance of creating habits and routine. *American Journal of Lifestyle Medicine, 13*(2), 142–144.

Beck, A. T., Freeman, A., & Associates. (1990). *Cognitive therapy of personality disorders.* New York: Guilford Press.

Blackboard. (2016). *Trends in community engagement: How K–12 schools are meeting the expectations of parents for digital communications.* Accessed at https://tomorrow.org/speakup/2016-digital-learning-reports-from-blackboard-and-speak-up.html on October 20, 2020.

BrainyQuote. (n.d.). *Theodore Roosevelt quotes.* Accessed at www.brainyquote.com/authors/theodore-roosevelt-quotes on March 1, 2021.

Centers for Disease Control and Prevention. (2012). *Parent engagement: Strategies for involving parents in school health.* Accessed at www.cdc.gov/healthyyouth/protective/pdf/parent_engagement_strategies.pdf on October 20, 2020.

Centers for Disease Control and Prevention. (2020a). *About the CDC-Kaiser ACE study.* Accessed at www.cdc.gov/violenceprevention/aces/about.html?CDC_AA_refVal=https%3A%2F%2Fwww.cdc.gov%2Fviolenceprevention%2Facestudy%2Fabout.html on March 23, 2021.

Centers for Disease Control and Prevention. (2020b). *Adverse childhood experiences (ACEs).* Accessed at www.cdc.gov/violenceprevention/acestudy on October 20, 2020.

Child Trends. (2018, September 16). *Parental involvement in schools.* Accessed at www.childtrends.org/?indicators=parental-involvement-in-schools on October 20, 2020.

Cobb, F., & Krownapple, J. (2019). *Belonging through a culture of dignity: The keys to successful equity implementation.* San Diego, CA: Mimi & Todd Press.

Cole, S. F., Eisner, A., Gregory, M., & Ristuccia, J. (2013). *Helping traumatized children learn: Creating and advocating for trauma-sensitive schools.* Boston: Massachusetts Advocates for Children.

Cook, A., Spinazzola, J., Ford, J., Lanktree, C., Blaustein, M., Cloitre, M., et al. (2005). Complex trauma in children and adolescents. *Psychiatric Annals, 35*(5), 390–398.

Covey, S. R. (2013). *The seven habits of highly effective people: Powerful lessons in personal change* (25th ed.). New York: Simon & Schuster.

Craig, S. E. (2016a). *Trauma-sensitive schools: Learning communities transforming children's lives, K–5.* New York: Teachers College Press.

Craig, S. E. (2016b). The trauma-sensitive teacher. *Educational Leadership, 74*(1), 28–32. Accessed at www.ascd.org/publications/educational_leadership/sept16/vol74/num01/The_Trauma-Sensitive_Teacher.aspx on October 20, 2020.

Crecco, J. (2017). The adverse childhood experiences (ACE) study: A hidden public health crisis. *Federation for Children with Special Needs.* Accessed at https://fcsn.org/newsletter/2017/august/ACE on April 15, 2021.

Curby, T. W., Rudasill, K. M., Edwards, T., & Pérez-Edgar, K. (2011). The role of classroom quality in ameliorating the academic and social risks associated with difficult temperament. *School Psychology Quarterly, 26*(2), 175–188.

Dearing, E., Kreider, H., Simpkins, S., & Weiss, H. B. (2006). Family involvement in school and low-income children's literacy: Longitudinal associations between and within families. *Journal of Educational Psychology, 98*(4), 653–664. Accessed at www.llss590fall2011.pbworks.com/w/file/fetch/45022608/Family%20involvement.pdf on October 21, 2020.

Downey, L. (2007). *Calmer classrooms: A guide to working with traumatised children.* Melbourne, Australia: Child Safety Commissioner. Accessed at www.acesconnection.com/g/aces-in-education/fileSendAction/fcType/5/fcOid/452934889391655998/fodoid/452934889391655997/Calmer%20Classrooms%20-%20A%20guide%20to%20working%20with%20traumatised%20children.pdf on October 21, 2020.

Duckworth, A. (2016). *Grit: The power of passion and perseverance.* New York: Scribner.

Duke University. (2017, December 1). Dropping out of high school linked to child abuse. *ScienceDaily.* Accessed at www.sciencedaily.com/releases/2017/12/171201131636.htm on February 27, 2021.

Dweck, C. S. (2008). *Mindset: The new psychology of success* (Updated ed.). New York: Random House.

Dweck, C. S. (2017). The journey to children's mindsets—and beyond. *Child Development Perspectives, 11*(2), 139–144.

Easterlin, M. C., Chung, P. J., Leng, M., & Dudovitz, R. (2019). Association of team sports participation with long-term mental health outcomes among individuals exposed to adverse childhood experiences. *JAMA Pediatrics, 173*(7), 681–688. Accessed at https://pubmed.ncbi.nlm.nih.gov/31135890/ on October 20, 2020.

Education Support. (2020). *Teacher Wellbeing Index 2020*. Accessed at www.educationsupport.org.uk/sites/default/files/teacher_wellbeing_index_2020.pdf on February 27, 2021.

Egger, H. L., & Angold, A. (2006). Common emotional and behavioral disorders in preschool children: Presentation, nosology, and epidemiology. *Journal of Child Psychology and Psychiatry, 47*(3–4), 313–337.

Eller, J. F., & Eller, S. A. (2009). *Creative strategies to transform school culture*. Thousand Oaks, CA: Corwin Press.

Eller, J. F., & Eller, S. A. (2011). *Working with difficult and resistant staff*. Bloomington, IN: Solution Tree Press.

Eller, J. F., & Eller, S. A. (2015). *Score to soar: Moving teachers from evaluation to professional growth*. Bloomington, IN: Solution Tree Press.

Eller, J. F., & Eller, S. A. (2016). *Thriving as a new teacher: Tools and strategies for your first year*. Bloomington, IN: Solution Tree Press.

Eller, J. F., & Eller, S. A. (2019). *Flip this school: How to lead the turnaround process*. Bloomington, IN: Solution Tree Press.

Engagement. (n.d.a). In *Merriam-Webster online*. Accessed at www.merriam-webster.com/dictionary/engagement on February 3, 2021.

Felitti, V. J. (2019) Origins of the ACE study. *American Journal of Preventive Medicine, 56*(6), 787–789.

Felitti, V., & Anda, R. (2009). *The adverse childhood experiences (ACE) study: Bridging the gap between childhood trauma and negative consequences later in life*. Accessed at www.acestudy.org on April 19, 2021.

Felitti, V., & Anda, R. (2010). The relationship of adverse childhood experiences to adult medical disease, psychiatric disorders and sexual behavior: Implications for healthcare. In R. Lanius, E. Vermetten, & C. Pain (Eds.), *The impact of early life trauma on health and disease: The hidden epidemic* (pp. 77–87). Cambridge, England: Cambridge University Press.

Ferlazzo, L. (2011). Involvement or engagement? *Educational Leadership, 68*(8), 10–14. Accessed at www.ascd.org/publications/educational-leadership/may11/vol68/num08/Involvement-or-Engagement%C2%A2.aspx on October 21, 2020.

Forbes, H. T. (2012). *Help for Billy: A beyond consequences approach to helping challenging children in the classroom*. Boulder, CO: Beyond Consequences Institute.

Gillihan, S. J. (2020, April 7). *The COVID-19 crisis may trigger emotions from past trauma* [Blog post]. Accessed at https://blogs.webmd.com/mental-health/20200407/the-covid19-crisis-may-trigger-emotions-from-past-trauma on March 3, 2021.

Ginott, H. G. (1972). *Teacher and child: A book for parents and teachers.* New York: Macmillan.

Goldstone, J. (Producer), & Jones, T. (Director). (1979). *Monty Python's life of Brian* [Motion picture]. England: Handmade Films.

Gough, P. B. (1991). Tapping parent power. *Phi Delta Kappan,* 72(5), 339.

Grand Rapids Public School District. (n.d.). *Parent engagement: Partnering together.* Accessed at www.grps.org/parents/parental-engagement on February 27, 2021.

Hammond, Z. (2015). *Culturally responsive teaching and the brain: Promoting authentic engagement and rigor among culturally and linguistically diverse students.* Thousand Oaks, CA: Corwin Press.

Harlacher, J. E. (2015). *Designing effective classroom managment.* Bloomington, IN: Marzano Resources.

Hawkins, J. D., Catalano, R. F., Kosterman, R., Abbott, R., & Hill, K. G. (1999). Preventing adolescent health-risk behaviors by strengthening protection during childhood. *Archives of Pediatrics & Adolescent Medicine, 153*(3), 226–234.

HelpGuide. (n.d.). *Helping children cope with traumatic events.* Accessed at https://helpguide.org/articles/ptsd-trauma/helping-children-cope-with-traumatic-stress.htm on April 15, 2021.

Henderson, A. T., & Berla, N. (Eds.). (1994). *A new generation of evidence: The family is critical to student achievement.* Washington, DC: National Committee for Citizens in Education.

Hierck, T. (2017). *Seven keys to a positive learning environment in your classroom.* Bloomington, IN: Solution Tree Press.

Hill, N. E., & Tyson, D. F. (2009). Parental involvement in middle school: A meta-analytic assessment of the strategies that promote achievement. *Developmental Psychology, 45*(3), 740–763. Accessed at www.ncbi.nlm.nih.gov/pmc/articles/PMC2782391 on October 21, 2020.

Involvement. (n.d.b). In *Merriam-Webster online.* Accessed at www.merriam-webster.com/dictionary/involvement on February 3, 2021.

Jensen, E. (2013). *Engaging students with poverty in mind: Practical strategies for raising achievement.* Alexandria, VA: Association for Supervision and Curriculum Development.

Jensen, E., & McConchie, L. (2020). *Brain-based learning: Teaching the way students really learn* (3rd ed.). Thousand Oaks, CA: Corwin Press.

Kohn, A. (2005). Unconditional teaching. *Educational Leadership, 63*(1), 20–24. Accessed at www.ascd.org/ASCD/pdf/journals/ed_lead/el200509_kohn.pdf on October 21, 2020.

Lu, W. (2017). Child and adolescent mental disorders and health care disparities: Results from the National Survey of Children's Health, 2011–2012. *Journal of Health Care for the Poor and Underserved, 28*(3), 988–1011.

Makri-Botsari, E. (2001). Causal links between academic intrinsic motivation, self-esteem, and unconditional acceptance by teachers in high school students. In R. J. Riding & S. G. Rayner (Eds.), *International perspectives on individual differences: Self perception* (Vol. 2, pp. 209–220). Westport, CT: Ablex.

Marzano, R. J. (2017). *The new art and science of teaching*. Bloomington, IN: Solution Tree Press.

Maslow, A. H. (1943). A theory of human motivation. *Psychological Review, 50*(4), 370–396.

Michigan Department of Education. (2015). *Collaborating for success: Parent engagement toolkit*. Accessed at https://michigan.gov/documents/mde/4a._Final_Toolkit_without_bookmarks_370151_7.pdf on January 22, 2021.

NASP School Safety and Crisis Response Committee. (2015). *Supporting students experiencing childhood trauma: Tips for parents and educators*. Bethesda, MD: National Association of School Psychologists. Accessed at www.nasponline.org/resources-and-publications/resources-and-podcasts/school-climate-safety-and-crisis/mental-health-resources/trauma/supporting-students-experiencing-childhood-trauma-tips-for-parents-and-educators on March 2, 2021.

National Center for Education Statistics. (2018). *Fast facts: Back to school statistics*. Accessed at https://nces.ed.gov/fastfacts/display.asp?id=372 on December 15, 2020.

National Center for Mental Health Promotion and Youth Violence Prevention. (2012). *Childhood trauma and its effects on healthy development*. Accessed at www.promoteprevent.org/sites/www.promoteprevent.org/files/resources/childhood%20trauma_brief_in_final.pdf on October 21, 2020.

National Child Traumatic Stress Network. (2017a). *Addressing race and trauma in the classroom: A resource for educators*. Los Angeles, CA, and Durham, NC: National Center for Child Traumatic Stress.

National Child Traumatic Stress Network. (2017b). *Family engagement and involvement in trauma mental health*. Accessed at www.nctsn.org/sites/default/files/resources/fact-sheet/cac_family_engagement_and_involvement_in_trauma_mental_health.pdf on February 28, 2021.

National Parent Teacher Association. (2000). *Building successful partnerships: A guide for developing parent and family involvement programs*. Bloomington, IN: National Educational Service.

National Scientific Council on the Developing Child. (2015). *Supportive relationships and active skill-building strengthen the foundations of resilience*. Cambridge, MA: Center on the Developing Child, Harvard University. Accessed at http://developingchild.harvard.edu/wp-content/uploads/2015/05/The-Science-of-Resilience.pdf on October 21, 2020.

Nealy-Oparah, S., & Scruggs-Hussein, T. C. (2018). *Trauma-informed leadership in schools: From the inside-out*. Accessed at https://schools4girlsofcolor.org/2018/01/trauma-informed-leadership on March 3, 2021.

Oehlberg, B. (2012). *Ending the shame: Transforming public education so it works for all students*. Pittsburgh, PA: RoseDog Books.

Organisation for Economic Co-operation and Development. (2020). *Parental involvement*. Accessed at https://gpseducation.oecd.org/revieweducationpolicies/#!node=41727&filter=all on February 28, 2021.

Park, D., Tsukayama, E., Yu, A., & Duckworth, A. L. (2020). The development of grit and growth mindset during adolescence. *Journal of Experimental Child Psychology, 198*, 104889.

Perry, B. D. (2016, December 13). The brain science behind student trauma. *Education Week*. Accessed at www.edweek.org/ew/articles/2016/12/14/the-brain-science-behind-student-trauma.html on October 21, 2020.

Rice, K. F., & Groves, B. M. (2005). *Hope and healing: A caregiver's guide to helping young children affected by trauma*. Washington, DC: Zero to Three.

Robbins, A. (1986). *Unlimited power: The new power of personal achievement*. New York: Free Press.

Roberts, M. (2019). *Enriching the learning: Meaningful extensions for proficient students in a PLC at Work*. Bloomington, IN: Solution Tree Press.

Schein, E. H. (2017). *Organizational culture and leadership* (5th ed.). Hoboken, NJ: Wiley.

Schickedanz, A., Halfon, N., Sastry, N., & Chung, P. J. (2018). Parents' adverse childhood experiences and their children's behavioral health problems. *Pediatrics, 142*(2). Accessed at https://pediatrics.aappublications.org/content/142/2/e20180023 on October 21, 2020.

Schwartz, H. L., Grant, D., Diliberti, M., Hunter, G. P., & Setodji, C. M. (2020) *Remote learning is here to stay: Results from the First American School District Panel survey*. Accessed at www.rand.org/pubs/research_reports/RRA956-1.html on February 28, 2021.

Sheldon, S. B., & Epstein, J. L. (2004). Getting students to school: Using family and community involvement to reduce chronic absenteeism. *School Community Journal, 14*(2), 39–56. Accessed at www.adi.org/journal/fw04/Sheldon%20&%20Epstein.pdf on October 21, 2020.

Sheldon, S. B., & Jung, S. B. (2015). *The family engagement partnership: Student outcome evaluation*. Accessed at www.pthvp.org/wp-content/uploads/2016/09/JHU-STUDY_FINAL-REPORT.pdf on October 21, 2020.

Significant 72. (2019). *What is #Significant72?* Accessed at www.significant72.com on October 20, 2020.

Souers, K., & Hall, P. (2016). *Fostering resilient learners: Strategies for creating a trauma-sensitive classroom*. Alexandria, VA: Association for Supervision and Curriculum Development.

Souers, K., & Hall, P. (2019). *Relationship, responsibility, and regulation: Trauma-invested practices for fostering resilient learners*. Alexandria, VA: Association for Supervision and Curriculum Development.

Sporleder, J., & Forbes, H. T. (2016). *The trauma-informed school: A step-by-step implementation guide for administrators and school personnel.* Boulder, CO: Beyond Consequences Institute.

Stamm, B. H., & Friedman, M. J. (2000). Cultural diversity in the appraisal and expression of trauma. In A. Y. Shalev, R. Yehuda, & A. C. McFarlane (Eds.), *The Plenum series on stress and coping: International handbook of human response to trauma* (pp. 69–85). Norwell, MA: Kluwer Academic.

State of Michigan. (n.d.). *Strategies for strong parent and family engagement.* Accessed at www.michigan.gov/documents/mde/file8culturep68_364183_7.pdf on October 21, 2020.

Teicher, M. H., Andersen, S. L., Polcari, A., Anderson, C. M., Navalta, C. P., & Kim, D. M. (2003). The neurobiological consequences of early stress and childhood maltreatment. *Neuroscience & Biobehavioral Reviews, 27*(1–2), 33–44.

Terrasi, S., & de Galarce, P. C. (2017). Trauma and learning in America's classrooms. *Phi Delta Kappan, 98*(6), 35–41.

Thomas, M. S., Crosby, S., & Vanderhaar, J. (2019). Trauma-informed practices in schools across two decades: An interdisciplinary review of research. *Review of Research in Education, 43*(1), 422–452.

Tremblay, R. E. (1999). When children's social development fails. In D. P. Keating & C. Hertzman (Eds.), *Developmental health and the wealth of nations: Social, biological, and educational dynamics* (pp. 55–71). New York: Guilford Press.

Van Tieu, H., & Koblin, B. A. (2009). HIV, alcohol, and noninjection drug use. *Current Opinion in HIV/AIDS, 4*(4), 314–318.

Wairimu, J. M., Macharia, S. M., & Muiru, A. (2016). Analysis of parental involvement and self-esteem on secondary school students in Kieni West Sub-County, Nyeri County, Kenya. *Journal of Education and Practice, 7*(27), 82–98. Accessed at https://files.eric.ed.gov/fulltext/EJ1115884.pdf on October 21, 2020.

Waterford.org. (2018). *How parent involvement leads to student success.* Accessed at www.waterford.org/education/how-parent-involvment-leads-to-student-success on December 15, 2020.

Watson, M. (2003). *Learning to trust: Transforming difficult elementary classrooms through developmental discipline.* San Francisco: Jossey-Bass.

WebMD. (2007). *TV violence: A cause of child anxiety and aggressive behavior?* Accessed at www.webmd.com/parenting/features/tv-violence-cause-child-anxiety-aggressive-behavior#1 on October 20, 2020.

Wilgoren, J. (2000, March 14). *Florida's vouchers a spur to two schools left behind.* Accessed at https://archive.nytimes.com/www.nytimes.com/library/national/031400voucher-edu.html on October 21, 2020.

Williams, K. C., & Hierck, T. (2015). *Starting a movement: Building culture from the inside out in professional learning communities.* Bloomington, IN: Solution Tree Press.

Wong, J. (2020, October 28). Teachers say return to school this fall has left them with overwhelming stress and a never-ending workload. *CBC-Canada*. Accessed at www.cbc.ca/news/canada/teacher-questionnaire-pandemic-1.5775805 on February 27, 2021.

Zenger, J., & Folkman, J. (2013, March 15). The ideal praise-to-criticism ratio. *Harvard Business Review*. Accessed at https://hbr.org/2013/03/the-ideal-praise-to-criticism on February 23, 2021.

Index

D

E

F

G

H

U

V

W

Y

Seven Keys to a Positive Learning Environment in Your Classroom
Tom Hierck
Creating a positive classroom learning environment is a complex but necessary task. By following the seven keys the author outlines, teachers can establish clearer expectations, enhance instruction and assessment practices, and foster quality relationships with students, maximizing the potential of all students.
BKF721

Uniting Academic and Behavior Interventions
Austin Buffum, Mike Mattos, Chris Weber, and Tom Hierck
Ensure students acquire the academic skills, dispositions, and knowledge necessary for long-term success. Examine what effective academic and behavior supports look like for all learners. Explore a step-by-step process for determining, targeting, and observing academic and behavior interventions.
BKF595

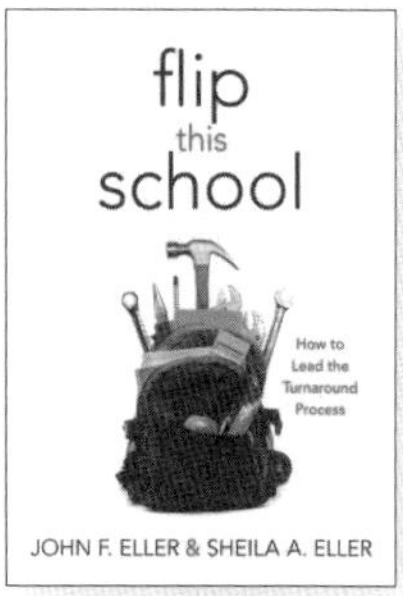

flip
this
school
How to Lead the Turnaround Process
JOHN F. ELLER & SHEILA A. ELLER

Flip This School
John F. Eller and Sheila A. Eller
Designed for administrators and teacher leaders, *Flip This School* presents a framework to lead a successful, sustainable school turnaround. Readers will gain a variety of practical strategies for planning school improvement efforts and collaborating with the existing staff to initiate a schoolwide transformation.
BKF669

score
to
soar
moving teachers from evaluation to professional growth
JOHN F. ELLER & SHEILA A. ELLER

Score to Soar
John F. Eller and Sheila A. Eller
Discover how to guide and enhance the job performance of teachers in your school or district. You'll learn how to evaluate teacher effectiveness, use multiple forms of data for evaluation, and communicate evaluation findings in a way that fosters professional growth.
BKF625

Solution Tree | Press a division of Solution Tree

Visit SolutionTree.com or call 800.733.6786 to order.